www.twinsisters.com

1-800-248-TWIN(8946)

Credits

Scripture taken from the HOLY BIBLE: NEW INTERNATIONAL VERSION®. NIV® Copyright 1973, 1978, 1984 by International Bible Society. Used by permission of Zondervan Bible Publishers.

Publisher: Twin Sisters Productions, LLC
Executive Producers: Kim Mitzo Thompson, Karen Mitzo Hilderbrand
All Songs Public Domain Except: *Jesus, I Love You; I Want to Walk With Jesus; I Want to Stop And Give My Lord Thanks; The Old Testament Song;* and *The New Testament Song* all with words and music by Kim Mitzo Thompson, Karen Mitzo Hilderbrand, Hal Wright.
Music Arranged By: Hal Wright
Workbook Author: Ken Carder
Graphic Design: Steven Dewitt

Twin 252CD
718451025229
ISBN-10: 1-57583-897-4
ISBN-13: 978-157583-897-7

© 2006 Twin Sisters IP, LLC. All Rights Reserved.
Printed in China.

Table of Contents

Introduction

Most kids love to sing! To hear them sings songs of praise and worship is so exciting. This new collection of Bible Songs features many classic choruses you may remember, hymns of the church too valuable not to share with the next generation of believers, and several new songs!

Scripture Spotlight provides a Biblical foundation for each song. Read and discuss the spotlight together then sing the song.

Praise Signs is a description of sign language movements for key words in each song. Signing helps children learn the words and the meaning. **Over 150 signs are included** in this book. Each sign is commonly accepted sign language—not just fun motions.

Puzzles, games, crafts, and activities reinforce the Biblical basis of each song. Each page is perfect for at-home learning and play or for the classroom!

Can you name the books of the Bible in order? Accept the challenge to **memorize the books of the Bible.** Together with your children learn *The Old Testament Song* and *The New Testament Song.* Then use the Pocket-sized Guide to the Books of the Bible to review at home, school, or church. Finally play Bible Book Builder to master the name and genre of each Bible book.

Scripture memory is any child's greatest defense today. Set a goal of each family member memorizing 30 scriptures. Use the **30 cut-out Scripture Memory cards.** Track each family member's progress on the **refrigerator-size Scripture Memory Chart.**

About the Author:

Ken Carder (Author, Editor)

Ken is a graduate of The University of Akron in Akron, OH with a B.A. in Communication And Rhetoric, and of Evangelical School of Theology in Myerstown, PA with a M.Div. Since 2001 Ken has worked exclusively with Twin Sisters Productions to develop new educational music resources for children. Ken is the Children's Pastor at Community Church of Portage Lakes (Akron, OH). He and his wife have worked extensively with young children in churches, summer camps, schools, a syndicated radio ministry broadcast, and community theater. Ken and his wife are proud parents of three children, Stephen, Nathan, and McKenna.

Praise Signs 101

Most kids love to do simple hand motions and choreography while they sing. The movements often make it much easier to memorize the words and more fun to perform. But the Praise Signs throughout this book are much more than fun hand motions. Kids will learn over 150 words in American Sign Language—a visual-gesture language developed by deaf people to communicate with each other. The visual-gestures learned early may motivate children to become proficient in sign language as adults.

- The following descriptions are used throughout this book:
  - **Closed Hand** – make a fist with your hand.
  - **Curved Hand** – your fingers are touching and curved slightly.
  - **Flat Hand** – your fingers are touching and held straight or flat.
  - **Open Hand** – your fingers are spread and held straight or flat.

- Most signs are made in the center of your body—between your shoulders and between your waist and top of your head.

- Signs dealing with the present time are made in front of your body. Signs dealing with the future use a forward movement away from your body. Signs dealing with the past move backward toward your body.

- Signs that deal with thoughts are usually made near your head. Signs that deal with emotions are made near your heart.

- When signing to music, try to express the key thought or meaning. Children may find it difficult if not impossible to sign every word and maintain the rhythm of the song. Feel free to add or omit signs to help to keep the flow of the song. Refer to the Praise Signs Index (pages 85-86) for additional key words that you might include.

- Finally, the Praise Signs are intended to be a primer or an introduction to signing. For more reference materials and training, visit your local library or search online.

Bible Songs

I'm Gonna Sing / Rejoice In The Lord Always

I'm gonna sing
    when the Spirit says, "Sing!"
I'm gonna sing
    when the Spirit says, "Sing!"
I'm gonna sing
    when the Spirit says, "Sing!"
And obey the Spirit of the Lord.

I'm gonna shout
    when the Spirit says, "Shout!"
I'm gonna shout
    when the Spirit says, "Shout!"
I'm gonna shout
    when the Spirit says, "Shout!"
And obey the Spirit of the Lord.

I'm gonna pray
    when the Spirit says, "Pray!"
I'm gonna pray
    when the Spirit says, "Pray!"
I'm gonna pray
    when the Spirit says, "Pray!"
And obey the Spirit of the Lord.

Rejoice in the Lord always,
And again I say rejoice!
Rejoice in the Lord always,
And again I say rejoice!
Rejoice, rejoice!
And again I say rejoice!
Rejoice, rejoice!
And again I say rejoice!

Scripture Spotlight

Philippians 4:4
Rejoice in the Lord always. I will say it again: Rejoice!

"I am so happy!" "Wow, that's great!" "I LOVE you!" "You're wonderful!" "Thank you!" Moms and dads say these to kids. Kids say them to moms and dads! When we feel so good about another person, we're happy to tell them how we feel.

But do we tell God how we feel about Him? What do you feel about His promise to never leave you alone? To always love you? To always forgive you? To always care for you? Tell God what you feel about Him right now.

Praise Signs

Use these simple movements as you worship with this song:

spirit: Pinch your thumb and index fingertips together on each hand. Spiral your left hand up and out.

sing: Bend your left arm in front of you. Swing your right hand back and forth over your left arm.

shout: Make a C with your right hand, close to your mouth, and bring your hand up and out.

pray: Fold your hands to pray.

rejoice: Brush the fingers of your right hand upward several times across your chest.

always: Point your index finger up and out. Circle it in a clockwise direction.

Joy, Joy, Joy!

Fill a bucket with water. Add quite a few table-tennis balls. Try to push them under the water.
What happens? The balls keep popping to the surface. Imagine that the balls are filled with the joy of knowing:

+ Jesus loves me no matter what.
+ Jesus is with me everywhere I go.
+ Jesus wants only the best for me!

+ Jesus will always forgive me.
+ Jesus is preparing a place for me in heaven.
+ Jesus will return one day and I can spend forever with Him!

Code Breaker

Use the code to learn why David sang songs to God.

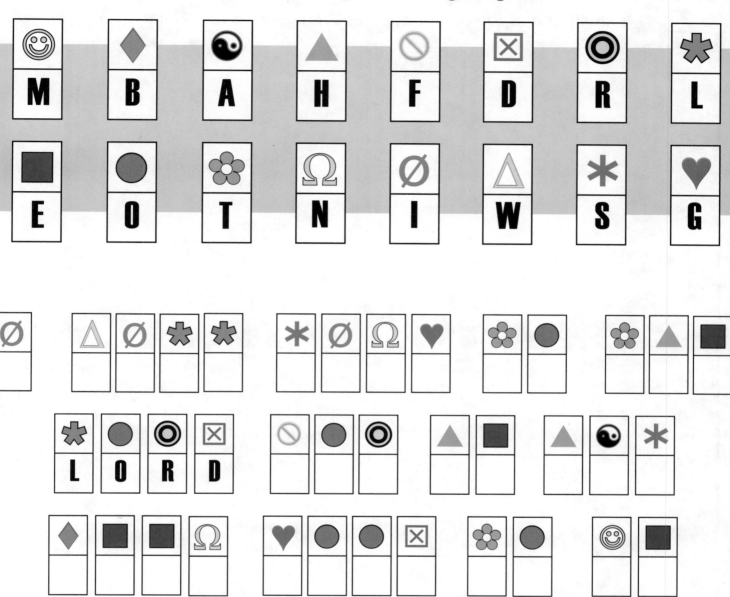

Psalm 13:6

You and I can sing to God for the same reason. On the next page, draw a picture that shows why you can sing songs to God.

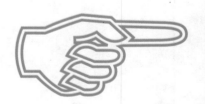

God Has Been Good To Me

I will sing to the Lord for he has been good to me. Psalm 13:6

Draw a picture that shows why you can sing songs to God.

Bible Songs

Come Bless The Lord / Jesus In The Morning

#2

Come bless the Lord,
all ye servants of the Lord
Who stand by night
in the house of the Lord!
Lift up your hands in the holy place
and bless the Lord,
And bless the Lord!

Jesus, Jesus,
Jesus in the morning,
Jesus in the noontime,
Jesus, Jesus,
Jesus when the sun goes down.

Praise Him, praise Him,
Praise Him in the morning,
Praise Him in the noontime,
Praise Him, praise Him,
Praise Him when the sun goes down.

Love Him, love Him,
Love Him in the morning,
Love Him in the noontime,
Love Him, love Him,
Love Him when the sun goes down.

Serve Him, serve Him,
Serve Him in the morning,
Serve Him in the noontime,
Serve Him, serve Him,
Serve Him when the sun goes down.

Thank Him, thank Him,
Thank Him in the morning,
Thank Him in the noontime,
Thank Him, thank Him,
Thank Him when the sun goes down.

Jesus, Jesus,
Jesus in the morning,
Jesus in the noontime,
Jesus, Jesus,
Jesus when the sun goes down.

Scripture Spotlight

Psalm 92:1-2
  It is good to praise the LORD
    and make music to your name, O Most High,
  ²to proclaim your love in the morning
    and your faithfulness at night.

Question: When is the right time to worship God?
Answer: ANYTIME!

Don't wait until Sunday to worship God! Here's your challenge: Every day this week when you hop out of bed in the morning, stop and say, "God, thank you for today!" At lunchtime, quietly say to yourself, "God, thank you for being with me this morning." Before going to sleep each night, talk to God and say, "I love you so much!" Do you accept this challenge?

Praise Signs

Use these simple movements as you worship with this song:

morning: Place your left hand in the bend of your right elbow. Bring your right flat hand toward self until upright, palm facing the body.

noontime: Point your left hand to the right, palm down; rest your right elbow on the back of your left hand, arm up, palm facing left.

evening: Hold your left hand flat, fingers pointing right. Place your right hand on the back of your left hand, fingers curved and pointing downward.

Jesus: Touch your left palm with your right middle finger; then touch your right palm with your left middle finger.

praise: Touch your right index finger to your mouth; then lightly clap your hands.

love: Cross your arms and bring them close to your chest .

serve: Hold both hands in front of your body with your palms facing up; alternate moving them back and forth.

thank: Touch the fingers of your right hand to your chin then bring them downward and outward.

Morning, Noon, and Night

Read Psalm 92:1-5 in your Bible. The writer says to proclaim—or talk about—God's love in the morning and God's faithfulness at night. Your challenge this week is to stop what you're doing for a few moments and worship God in the morning, at lunchtime, and again at nighttime. Use this chart to help you remember. Put a sticker, draw a picture, or write a few words in each square when you have stopped to worship God.

	Morning	Noon	Night
Monday			
Tuesday			
Wednesday			
Thursday			
Friday			
Saturday			
Sunday			

Bible Songs

Praise Him, Praise Him; Hallelu, Hallelu #3

Praise Him, praise Him,
        all ye little children.
God is love. God is love.
Praise Him, praise Him,
        all ye little children.
God is love. God is love.

Serve Him, serve Him,
        all ye little children.
God is love. God is love.
Serve Him, serve Him,
        all ye little children.
God is love. God is love.

Love Him, love Him,
        all ye little children.
God is love. God is love.
Love Him, love Him,
        all ye little children.
God is love. God is love.

Hallelu, Hallelu,
Hallelu, Hallelujah!
Praise ye the Lord!
Hallelu, Hallelu,
Hallelu, Hallelujah!
Praise ye the Lord!

Praise ye the Lord.
Hallelujah!
Praise ye the Lord.
Hallelujah!
Praise ye the Lord.
Hallelujah!
Praise ye the Lord!

Scripture Spotlight

Psalm 8:2
From the lips of children and infants you have ordained praise...

God LOVES when kids like you worship Him! Imagine God smiling when He hears you sing a favorite Bible song or when you say, "God, I love you!" Most kids are excited to worship God. They sing loud and pray simply. That brings a smile to God's face. In fact, God encourages adults to be more like kids.

Praise Signs

Use these simple movements as you worship with this song:

praise: Touch your right index finger to your mouth, then lightly clap your hands.

serve: Hold both hands in front of your body with your palms facing up; alternate moving them back and forth.

love: Cross your arms and bring them close to your chest.

children: Pretend to pat the heads of children with both hands, palms down.

hallelujah: Clap once; then hold up both closed hands with your thumb and index fingertips touching. Make small circular movements.

Code Breaker

One day, Jesus' closest friends thought Jesus would not want to spend time with children. His friends tried to send the children away. Find out what Jesus said to the children. Starting with the letter L, circle every other letter. Write the circled letters in the spaces below. Read Luke 18:15-17 in your Bible.

LMEFTMTOHREYLJIMTVTB
LRESCQHZIVLTDNRMERNS
CTOYMREBTNOTMVEXDRO
MNYTMKVEBEYPATQHWEJ
MKARWTASY

" _ _ _ _ _ _ _ _ _ _ _ _ _ _ _ _ _ _
_ _ _ _ _ _ _ _ _ _ _ ," " HE SAID.
" _ _ _ _ , " _ _ _ _ _ _ _ _ _ _ _ . "

"Let the Children Come to Me!" Tag

Play this game with a group of friends. Players race to come to Jesus, trying not to be tagged by a "disciple."

Tie together the ends of a very long rope and lay it in a circle. Place a chair in the center of the circle to represent Jesus. If you want, choose one player to be "Jesus" and sit in the chair. Choose another player to be a "disciple," and have the disciple stand inside the circle. The other players gather outside the circle. Explain that you will call on one or two players at a time to race to Jesus. When called players lift up the rope and try to sneak under it to race to Jesus. The disciple will try to tag the players. Tagged players sit down where they were tagged and can be freed when another player taps them on their way to Jesus. Players run back outside the circle after touching the chair.

Afterward, use the following questions to discuss Luke 18:15-17.

1. How did it feel while you were waiting to be called to race to Jesus?

2. How did it feel being tagged and not being allowed to reach Jesus?

3. Why do you think the disciples wanted to keep the children away from Jesus?

4. Why do you think Jesus invited the children to come visit with him?

5. What do you think Jesus said to the children?

Bible Songs

Jesus, I Love You #4

Just watch me clap, clap, clap, clap
        clap my hands in praise.
Just watch me stomp, stomp, stomp, stomp
        stomp my feet and say
Jesus, I love you.
You're my Savior,
        this is true.
Jesus, I love you
so I'll worship only you.
Jesus, Jesus I love you.
Jesus, Jesus I love you.
Jesus, Jesus I love you.
I love you.

Scripture Spotlight

Acts 3:8
He jumped to his feet and began to walk. Then he went with them into the temple courts, walking and jumping, and praising God.

Men and women were pushing their way through the noisy crowds going to the temple. All at once the people heard happy shouts and laughter and joy. Nearly everyone stopped and looked around. Soon they saw one man walking and jumping and praising God. The man was so happy. He stopped and hugged two of Jesus' friends. And then he continued to walk and jump and praise God. Read Acts 3:1-9 and find out why the man was so happy!

Praise Signs

Use these simple movements as you worship with this song:

clap: Lightly clap your hands!

praise: Touch your right index finger to your mouth, then lightly clap your hands.

Jesus: Touch your left palm with your right middle finger; then touch your right palm with your left middle finger.

I love you: Hold your right hand up with palm facing forward. Extend only your thumb, index, and little fingers.

worship: Close your left hand over your right closed hand and move them slowly toward yourself.

you: Point your index finger forward; make a sweeping motion from left to right.

TIP: Tracks 2, 3, and 4 flow together as a great worship set!

Jump Rope Praise

Challenge players to jump rope as long as they can. Learn this rhyme together. Each player jumps and counts to the rhyme as long as possible. You may limit the number if you have great jumpers! All kids can count together.

I praise you, Jesus, yes I do.
You love me and I love you.
I'll count to ten and say it again:
I Love You!

Walking and Jumping and Praising God!

One day a man was walking and jumping and praising God in the temple. Help the man find his way from the temple and to his home. Read why the man was so happy in Acts 3:1-9

Start

End

Bible Songs

#5

Bless The Lord, O My Soul

Bless the Lord, O my soul
Bless the Lord, O my soul
Let all that is within me
bless his holy name.

Scripture Spotlight

Psalm 103:1
Praise the LORD, O my soul; all my inmost being, praise his holy name.

When a crowd of people is standing and cheering, it's easy for us to stand and cheer too. Often you and I do something just because everyone else is doing that same thing. That's not always bad. But God wants our worship to be personal. He wants YOU to worship HIM. Read Psalm 103:1-5. In these verses the psalm writer uses the word "my" not "ours." Next time you sing or talk to God, don't just think or say what everyone is thinking or saying. Make your worship personal by saying to God what YOU really think and feel about Him.

In verse 2 what does the psalm writer say you and I should remember?

Praise Signs

Use these simple movements as you worship with this song:

bless: Make a fist with both hands, thumbs up. Lightly touch your thumbs to your chin, open and move both hands downward and forward, palms down.

Lord: Make an L with your right hand near your left shoulder. Bring it down near your right waist.

soul: Make a fist with your right hand, thumb side up. Pinch the thumb and index fingertips together on the your hand and spiral the left hand up.

name: Put your index and middle fingers together on both hands. Tap both hands together.

all: Hold your left flat front in front, palm facing your body. Move your right flat hand, palm facing out, around your left hand. End with the back of your right hand in the palm of your left hand.

me: Point your right index finger toward the chest.

Praise Potato

Players stand or sit in a circle. Play praise music while players pass a foam ball or a stuffed animal. When the music stops, the player with the object must say one thing for which he or she is thankful.

Bless the Lord A, B, C

King David said, "I will praise the Lord. I won't forget anything he does for me." (Psalm 103:3 NIrV) You and I can bless the Lord by remembering all the good things God does. For each letter of the alphabet, think of something good God did in the past, is doing now, or will do for you in the future. When you're done, say the list out loud to God.

A _____

B _____

C _____

D _____

E _____

F _____

G _____

H _____

I _____

J _____

K _____

L _____

M _____

N _____

O _____

P _____

Q _____

R _____

S _____

T _____

U _____

V _____

W _____

X _____

Y _____

Z _____

Bible Songs
Scripture Spotlight

Heavenly Father, I Appreciate You; God Is So Good

#6

Heavenly Father,
    I appreciate You.
Heavenly Father,
    I appreciate You.
I love You, adore You.
    I bow down before You.
Heavenly Father,
    I appreciate You.

Son of God,
    what a wonder You are.
Son of God,
    what a wonder You are.
You've cleansed me from sin,
    sent Your Spirit within.
Son of God,
    what a wonder You are.

Holy Spirit,
    what a comfort You are.
Holy Spirit,
    what a comfort You are.
You lead us. You guide us.
    You live right inside us.
Holy Spirit,
    what a comfort You are.

God is so good.
God is so good.
God is so good.
He's so good to me.

I love Him so.
I love Him so.
I love Him so.
He's so good to me.

I praise His name.
I praise His name.
I praise His name.
He's so good to me.

Psalm 107:1
Give thanks to the LORD, for he is good; his love endures forever.

Ten poor men were found alone on the city streets. One afternoon a stranger approached the men and gave each one a very, very special gift. Holding their gift, each man quickly turned, ran down the street and out of sight. Soon the stranger was standing alone on the sidewalk. A few moments later, the stranger looked up. One of the poor men was running back holding the gift in his hands. Reaching the stranger, the poor man stopped, placed the gift on the ground, and gave the stranger a bear-hug. With small tears in his eyes, the poor man was simply saying, "Thank you! Thank you so much!" Now, think. How many men received a special gift from the stranger? How many men thought to say, "Thank you"?

This happened to Jesus. He made ten very sick men well again. Only one man stopped to say, "Thank you" to Jesus. Read it for yourself in your Bible: Luke 17:11-19

Praise Signs

Use these simple movements as you worship with this song:

Heavenly Father: Point your right index finger upward. Move your hand back and down, fingers pointing up, palm left.

I: Point your right index finger toward your chest.

appreciate: Circle your heart with your right middle finger.

you: Point your right index finger forward; make a sweeping motion from left to right.

I love you: Hold your right hand up with palm facing forward. Extend only your thumb, index, and little fingers.

adore (worship): Close your left hand over your right closed hand and move them slowly toward yourself.

bow down: Stand and kneel your right middle and index fingers on the palm of your left hand.

Holy Spirit: Pinch your thumb and index fingertips together on each hand. Spiral your left hand up and out.

guide: Grasp your left fingertips with your right hand and lead your left hand forward.

us: Touch your right index finger on your right shoulder; then move it in a semi-circle until it touches your left shoulder.

inside: Make an L with both hands by pointing your index fingers down and thumbs up; move both hands up from your waist.

good: Place the fingers of your right flat hand at your lips then move the hand down into the palm of your left hand.

Thankfulness: True or False

Read each sentence. Circle the T if the sentence is true (right).
Circle the F is the sentence is false (wrong). Read the sentences
to your friends and find out what they know about being thankful.

God only wants me to thank Him on Thanksgiving Day.	**T**	**F**
Some days I have no reason to thank God.	**T**	**F**
God knows I'm thankful. I don't have to tell Him.	**T**	**F**
There is more than one way to thank God.	**T**	**F**
God is the giver of every good and perfect gift.	**T**	**F**
I only need to thank God for things I can see—like clothes, food, cars, houses, and people.	**T**	**F**

Thanksgiving Jumble

Read Psalm 100:4-5 in your Bible. Number the
following words and phrases in the correct order.

gates with	praise;	his love
_____	_____	_____

to him	his name.	Enter His
_____	_____	_____

is good and	and his	forever.
_____	_____	_____

give thanks	courts with	For the LORD
_____	_____	_____

endures	and praise	thanksgiving
_____	_____	_____

Remember Rocks

God stopped the Jordan River from flowing so His people could walk across the river on dry ground into the land God had promised to give them. God told Joshua to send twelve men back into the river. Each man picked up a large rock from the middle of the river and carried it back to the shore. That night the 12 rocks were carefully placed in the camp. Whenever the children and adults saw the rocks God said to remember how good and mighty He is. Read what happened in your own Bible: Joshua 4:1-9

Make your own Remember Rocks. On each rock below draw or write how God has been good to you and your family.

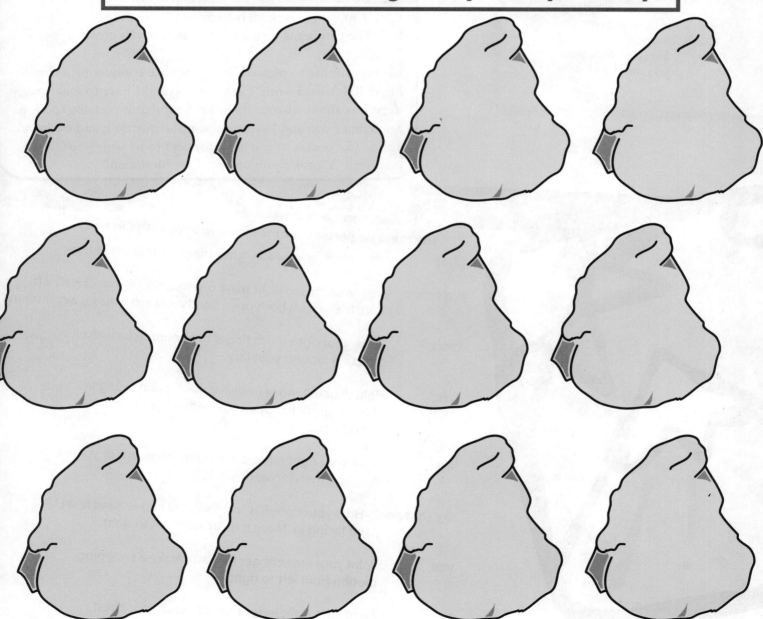

Bible Songs
Scripture Spotlight

Climb, Climb Up Sunshine Mountain

#7

Climb, climb up
　　Sunshine Mountain,
　　heavenly breezes blow.
Climb, climb up
　　Sunshine Mountain,
　　faces all aglow.
Turn, turn your
　　face from doubting,
　　look up into the sky.
Climb, climb up
　　Sunshine Mountain,
　　you and I.

Philippians 3:14
I press on toward the goal to win the prize for which God has called me heavenward in Christ Jesus.

Have you or someone you know ever made it to the top of a climbing wall at school, a carnival or an amusement park? Climbers are strapped in very carefully. The climber puts one foot on a foothold and stretches to reach another climbing hold. Then the climber pulls her body up and decides which climbing holds to reach for next. Sometimes the climber slips and falls backward a bit, but starts up again. Climbing is harder than it appears. The goal is to make it to the top and ring the bell. The climber is then lowered safely to the ground.

Living your life to please God is a lot like conquering a climbing wall. It's hard work. Each day you and I have to make many decisions about what to do or say next that is pleasing to God. Sometimes you and I slip up and make mistakes, and we begin again. The goal is to reach the top and to be with Jesus. Keep climbing! "Climb, climb up Sunshine Mountain!"

Praise Signs

Use these simple movements as you worship with this song:

climb: With palms facing each other, make a climbing motion.

mountain: Strike your closed right hand on the back of your closed left hand; then move both open hands upward with a wavy motion.

faces: Move your right index finger in a counterclockwise direction around your face.

turn: Hold your left index finger upward, palm facing in. Move your right index finger around your left index finger in counterclockwise circles.

look: Point your right middle and index fingertips at your eyes and then forward.

sky (heavens): Hold your right flat hand slightly above head level, palm facing in. Move it in arc from left to right.

you: Point your index finger forward; make a sweeping motion from left to right.

I: Point your right index finger toward your chest.

Sunshine Mountain Climber

You'll need:
- Construction paper or poster board
- A straw
- 2 beads
- String
- Paper towel tube
- Scissors
- Stapler
- Crayons, markers, and craft supplies

 step 1

First, draw your Sunshine Mountain climber on a piece of construction paper or poster board. Make sure your climber has arms because this is how it holds on to the strings. Now cut out the climber and color it. Make sure you color the backs of the arms.

 **step 2**

Next, cut two 1-inch pieces of straw. Tape a straw piece onto the middle of each of the climber's arms. Now, fold the arms over the straw pieces and staple them in place. The body is now complete.

 **step 3**

Now, cut two long pieces of string. Tie the ends of the strings around a paper towel tube. Thread the string through the straw pieces on the climber's arms, and tie a bead onto the end of each of the strings.

 **step 4**

To hang up your climber, cut one short piece of string and tie it around the middle of the tube. Hang the climber on a door hinge or coat hook. Slide the climber to the bottom of the string.

 **step 5**

Pull the strings one at a time and your climber will climb up the string! When you pull on the right string the climber should slide up the right side until it gets stuck. And when you pull on the left string, it should climb up the left side until it gets stuck.

Bible Songs
Scripture Spotlight

#8

The Happy Day Express

We're going to a mansion on
   the Happy Day Express.
The letters on the engine
   spell J-E-S-U-S.
The guard calls,
   "All for heaven."
We gladly answer, "Yes!"
We're going to the mansion on
   the Happy Day Express.

You're welcome to the mansion
   on the Happy Day Express.
The way to come is just to
   trust in J-E-S-U-S.
So hear the call from heaven
   and gladly answer, "Yes!"
Come with us to the mansion
   on the Happy Day Express.

John 14:6
Jesus answered, "I am the way and the truth and the life. No one comes to the Father except through me."

Not too long ago more people traveled across our country on railroad trains than in airplanes. In some big cities, the travelers came to the train station where many trains were lined up. The passengers waited in the train station for the conductor to announce where the trains were going. One train was going to New York City. Another train was going to Chicago. Another train might be going to Washington D.C. When the passengers heard the announcement, they would walk to the right train, show the conductor their tickets, get on the train, and find their seats. Eventually the passengers reached their destinations.

This fun Bible song reminds me that going to heaven is somewhat like riding a train. We know heaven is the destination—where we want to go. Believing that Jesus is the Son of God is like the ticket passengers must show to the conductor on a train. Each day of our life is like a train ride that will one day lead us to heaven. "Welcome to the mansion on the Happy Day Express!"

Praise Signs

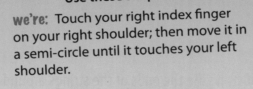

Use these simple movements as you worship with this song:

we're: Touch your right index finger on your right shoulder; then move it in a semi-circle until it touches your left shoulder.

go: Point both index fingers toward each other and rotate them around each other moving away from your body.

mansion (house): Form the point of a triangle at head level with both flat hands; move them apart and straight down, fingers pointing up.

Jesus: Touch your left palm with your right middle finger; then touch your right palm with your left middle finger.

calls (says): Make a small forward circular movent in front of your mouth with your right index finger pointed left.

heaven: Hold both hands in front, fingers pointing up, palms facing your body. Move both hands in a circle and end with your hands crossed at your forehead.

yes: Nod your right closed hand, palm forward.

you're: Point your index finger forward; make a sweeping motion from left to right.

welcome: Hold your right flat hand to your right, palm facing left. Sweep your hand toward your body.

come: Point both index fingers toward each other and rotate them around each other simultaneously, moving toward your body.

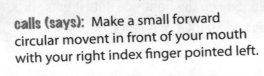

The Happy Day Express

Make copies of this page for your family or classroom. Cut out and color the engine. Cut out a train car for each family member or student. Each person colors a train car and writes his or her name along the bottom. Display The Happy Day Express engine, train cars, and caboose at home or in your classroom.

The Happy Day Express
Jesus

The Happy Day Express
Heaven

Bible Songs
Scripture Spotlight

#9

Happy All The Time

I'm in-right,
 out-right,
 up-right,
 down-right
happy all the time.

I'm in-right,
 out-right,
 up-right,
 down-right
happy all the time.

Since Jesus Christ came in
And cleansed my heart
 from sin.
I'm in-right,
 out-right,
 up-right,
 down-right
happy all the time.

James 5:13
Is any one of you in trouble? He should pray. Is anyone happy? Let him sing songs of praise.

This song brings a smile to my face. I remember singing this song as a little boy! All the kids would always lean forward on the word "in-right;" lean backward on the word "out-right;" stretch tall on the word "up-right" and squat low on the word "down right". Then, we would speed the song and movements up faster and faster until everyone fell into giggles. As a leader, I remember challenging other kids to sing the song as fast I would sing. And then I would say the first line, mumble the other lines, say the last words, and claim to be finished. We had so much fun! Those were happy times.

This fun action song reminds me to be happy knowing that Jesus loves me. Don't worry! Be happy!

Praise Signs

Use these simple movements as you worship with this song:

happy: Move both flat hands in forward circular movements with palms touching your chest alternately.

Jesus: Touch your left palm with your right middle finger; then touch your right palm with your left middle finger.

heart: Place your right flat hand over your heart with your fingers extended.

cleanse (pardon): Stroke the lower part of your left flat hand several times with your right fingertips.

sin: Point both index fingers toward each other with palms facing your body. Move them simultaneously in a circle—up, out, down, and back together.

Who is Happy?

Jesus taught a large group of people while on a small mountainside. He taught the people how to be happy. Read Jesus' words in Matthew 5:1-12. Substitute the word "happy" for the word "blessed."

The last part of each sentence is mixed up. Unscramble the letters of each word. Rearrange the words in the correct order and discover what Jesus said. Read Matthew 5:1-12 again if you need help.

Blessed are the poor in spirit, for theirs   fo neveah dmogink si eht

Blessed are those who mourn, for they   eb dterofmco liwl

Blessed are the meek, for they   eth thrae liwl triehni

Blessed are those who hunger and
thirst for righteousness, for they   dellif lliw eb

Blessed are the merciful, for they   wlli eb cymre hswno

Blessed are the pure in heart, for they   dGo llwi ese

Blessed are the peacemakers, for they   eb nsso fo llecad Gdo

Blessed are those who are persecuted
because of righteousness for theirs   het nvehae mogknid si fo

Bible Songs

I Am A C-H-R-I-S-T-I-A-N; Down In My Heart

#10

I am a C, I am a C-H,
I am a C-H-R-I-S-T-I-A-N,
And I have C-H-R-I-S-T in my H-E-A-R-T
And I will L-I-V-E E-T-E-R-N-A-L-L-Y.

I've got the joy, joy, joy, joy down in my heart,
Down in my heart, Down in my heart.
I've got the joy, joy, joy, joy down in my heart,
Down in my heart to stay.

I've got the love of Jesus,
          love of Jesus down in my heart,
          Down in my heart,
          down in my heart.
I've got the love of Jesus,
          love of Jesus down in my heart,
Down in my heart to stay.

And I'm so happy, so very happy.
I've got the love of Jesus
          in my heart, down in my heart.
And I'm so happy, so very happy.
I've got the love of Jesus
          in my heart!

I've got the Peace that passes
understanding down in my heart,
          Down in my heart,
          down in my heart.
I've got the Peace that passes
understanding down in my heart,
Down in my heart to stay.

And I'm so happy, so very happy.
I've got the love of Jesus
          in my heart, down in my heart.
And I'm so happy, so very happy.
I've got the love of Jesus
          in my heart!

Scripture Spotlight

John 3:16
For God so loved the world that he gave his one and only Son, that whoever believes in him shall not perish but have eternal life.

Forever is a long, long time. Sometimes it's hard to understand "forever." When it's January and you're waiting for school to end in June, it seems like "forever" until the last day of school! It's just a week until your birthday but it seems like "forever" until the birthday party begins. In the Bible, the words "eternity" and "eternal" are the same as saying "forever."

Now, read John 3:16. What is the next to the last word in John 3:16? Read the verse again but use the word "forever" instead of the word "eternal."

Now, "forever life" doesn't sound quite right, I know. But it still helps us to understand that Jesus wants you and me to have a "forever life" with Him. Can you imagine living with Jesus forever?

Praise Signs

Use these simple movements as you worship with this song:

Christian: Touch your left palm with your right middle finger; then touch your right palm with your left middle finger; then with both palms facing each other, make a straight downward movement

Jesus: Touch your left palm with your right middle finger; then touch your right palm with your left middle finger.

heart: Place your right flat hand over your heart with your fingers extended.

live: Make an L with both hands by pointing your index fingers down and thumbs up; move both hands up from your waist.

forever: Circle your right index finger in a clockwise direction, palm up; then extend your thumb and little finger and move your hand forward.

A C-H-R-I-S-T-I-A-N Hands Down!

Cut out each letter card. Lay them faceup in any order on a table. Try to sing "I Am A C- H-R-I-S -T-I-A-N" slapping each letter as you say it! Time yourself! Then, play the game with several friends, assigning one or two letters to each friend. Make copies of this page and play with teams.

C H R I

S T L A

N V E Y

Scripture Spotlight

#10

I Am A C-H-R-I-S-T-I-A-N; Down In My Heart

I am a C, I am a C-H,
I am a C-H-R-I-S-T-I-A-N,
And I have C-H-R-I-S-T in my H-E-A-R-T
And I will L-I-V-E E-T-E-R-N-A-L-L-Y.

I've got the joy, joy, joy, joy down in my heart,
Down in my heart, Down in my heart.
I've got the joy, joy, joy, joy down in my heart,
Down in my heart to stay.

I've got the love of Jesus,
   love of Jesus down in my heart,
   Down in my heart,
   down in my heart.
I've got the love of Jesus,
   love of Jesus down in my heart,
Down in my heart to stay.

And I'm so happy, so very happy.
I've got the love of Jesus
   in my heart, down in my heart.
And I'm so happy, so very happy.
I've got the love of Jesus
   in my heart!

I've got the Peace that passes
   understanding down in my heart,
   Down in my heart,
      down in my heart.
I've got the Peace that passes
   understanding down in my heart,
Down in my heart to stay.

And I'm so happy, so very happy.
I've got the love of Jesus
   in my heart, down in my heart.
And I'm so happy, so very happy.
I've got the love of Jesus
   in my heart!

Philippians 4:7
And the peace of God, which transcends all understanding, will guard your hearts and your minds in Christ Jesus.

The word "heart" is hard to understand. When we sing, "I've got the joy, joy, joy, joy down in my heart" we're not talking about the heart inside our body that pumps blood. Have you ever heard someone say, "Let's get to the heart of the matter"? They want to understand the most important part of something. When you say, "I love my puppy with all my heart" you're saying that you really, really, really, really love your puppy. Or maybe someone wants to take you "to the heart of town"—the center of business or activity in your city. When you think of the word "heart" you're really talking about the most important part of you—your mind and your feelings. So when you sing, "I've got the joy, joy, joy down in my heart" you're trying say that deep inside you, the best part of you, you're happy—because God loves you!

Praise Signs

Use these simple movements as you worship with this song:

joy/happy: Move both flat hands in forward circular movements with palms alternately touching your chest .

down: Point your right index finger down with palm facing in, and push it down slightly.

heart: Place your right flat hand over your heart with your fingers extended.

happy: Move both flat hands in forward circular movements with palms touching your chest alternately.

peace: Place your right flat hand just above your left flat hand at chest level; pushboth hands down slightly.

have (got): Place the fingertips of both curved hands on your chest.

Guard Your Heart

You'll need a cut-out heart for each player. Players help one another tape a heart in the middle of their back. To play, players spread throughout the game area. On 'GO!' players are to "guard their hearts" while trying to collect other players' hearts. The game can get rough, so be careful. When time is up, count how many hearts players have collected. Most players will assume the real object of the game is to collect the most hearts—but that's not what you said! Announce that the real winners are those who still have their heart, regardless of how many—if any—hearts they collected! Most players who "Guarded Your Heart" probably collected none or only a few other hearts. After the game, ask the following questions: Was it easier to guard your heart or to take another player's heart? In real life, what can sometimes take away your "heart"?

A Clean Heart

Mark off a large heart on the floor with masking tape or a rope. Scatter many items of various sizes and shapes inside the heart. Explain that the items represent "sin" in our lives. Divide players into two teams. Teams stand far away from the heart. On your signal, the first player from each team runs into the heart, removes one item, and runs back to the team. The next player in line takes his or her turn. Play continues until all the "sin" is removed. The team with the most sin removed from the heart is the winner. After the game discuss how we sometimes view sin: big sins and small sins. God doesn't measure sin that way.

Bible Songs
Scripture Spotlight

#11

Oh Be Careful, Little Eyes

Oh be careful little eyes
    what you see!
Oh be careful little eyes
    what you see!
For the Father up above
    is looking down in love.
Oh be careful little eyes
    what you see!

Oh be careful little ears
    what you hear!
Oh be careful little ears
    what you hear!
For the Father up above
    is looking down in love.
Oh be careful little ears
    what you hear!

Oh be careful little hands
    what you do!
Oh be careful little hands
    what you do!
For the Father up above
    is looking down in love.
Oh be careful little hands
    what you do!

Oh be careful little feet
    where you go!
Oh be careful little feet
    where you go!
For the Father up above
    is looking down in love.
Oh be careful little feet
    where you go!

Ephesians 5:15
Be very careful, then, how you live—not as unwise but as wise...

Think about the last time you were in trouble. Why did you get in trouble? Did you see someone doing something wrong and think, "I can do that too"? Or maybe you continued to listen to music that your parents don't allow you to listen to. Did you get angry, raise your hands and try to hit your brother? Maybe you went someplace that is off-limits. Your eyes, ears, hands, and feet can very easily get you in trouble.

God is aware of what you do with our eyes, ears, hands, and feet. He's not watching you hoping that you get in trouble—like a little brother or sister waiting to tattle on you! No, God's watching you because He loves you. He DOESN'T want you to get in trouble! He doesn't want you to get hurt. You and I should learn to stop and think, "God's watching. What should I do?"

Praise Signs

Use these simple movements as you worship with this song:

careful: Cross and lightly tap both wrists while making a V with your index and middle fingers.

eyes: Point to your eye with your right index finger.

Father (God):   Place your right flat hand over your heart with your fingers extended.

looking: Point your right middle and index fingertips at your eyes and then forward.

love: Cross your arms and bring them close to your chest.

ears: Touch or point to your right ear with your right index finger.

hands: Lightly tap the back of each hand.

feet: Point first to one foot and then the other.

God's Eye

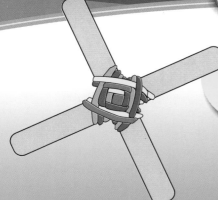

Make this traditional "God's Eye" as a reassuring reminder that "God is looking down in love." Read Psalm 139

You'll need:
- Two craft sticks or twigs
- Glue
- Yarn in several different colors
- Scissors

1. Glue two craft sticks or twigs together in a cross.
2. Take one color of yarn and wrap it over and around one stick, then over and around the next, over and around the next, and so on. Keep doing that until the color is used up.
3. Tie a different color string onto the old one with a tight knot.
4. Repeat steps 2 + 3 until complete.
5. Tie or glue a small piece of yarn to the top of your God's Eye. Hang your God's Eye where you will see it throughout the day.

Tangled Up

Players stand in a circle with their arms stretched out in front of them. With all of the hands in the middle, players move toward the center of the circle and grab two other hands in the center (not a person next to them). The group will be in one big knot. Players try to untangle themselves without letting go of anyone's hand. After the game, talk about how easy it is to become entangled in wrong behaviors and how difficult it is to free ourselves.

Don't Fall Into Sin

Place sheets of construction paper on the floor all around the room, far enough apart that players have to take big steps to move from one sheet to another. Players stand in a line and hold hands. Explain that the papers are the safety area. The rest of the floor is "sin." Holding hands with the person in front and behind, players walk around the room. Discuss how easy or difficult was it to stay on the paper, what it felt like to fall into "sin," or how players helped one another.

Bible Songs

Give Me Oil In My Lamp

Give me oil in my lamp.
Keep me burning, burning, burning.
Give me oil in my lamp, I pray.
Give me oil in my lamp.
Keep me burning, burning, burning.
Keep me burning 'til the break of day.

Sing Hosanna, sing Hosanna,
Sing Hosanna to the King of Kings!
Sing Hosanna, sing Hosanna,
Sing Hosanna to the King.

Give me joy in my heart.
Keep me praising, praising, praising.
Give me joy in my heart, I pray.
Give me joy in my heart.
Keep me praising, praising, praising!
Keep me praising 'til the break of day.

Make me a fisher of men.
Keep me seeking, seeking, seeking.
Make me a fisher of men, I pray.
Make me a fisher of men.
Keep me seeking, seeking, seeking
Keep me seeking 'til the break of day.

Give me love in my heart.
Keep me serving, serving, serving.
Give me love in my heart, I pray.
Give me love in my heart.
Keep me serving, serving, serving.
Keep me serving 'til the break of day

Scripture Spotlight

Matthew 25:13
Therefore keep watch, because you do not know the day or the hour.

Ask an adult if they've ever run out of gasoline while driving a car. The car sputters, slows down, and then stops completely. The only way to start the car again is to add more gasoline. Maybe you've seen someone walking along the highway toward a gas station.

Jesus told a story of ten women with oil lamps. One night all ten women went out to wait for a very special guest to come. Five women had enough oil to keep their lamps burning for a very long time. But the other five women did not have enough oil: their lamps burned out. Jesus explained that He was the special guest. We must be prepared to wait for a very long time for Jesus to come and take us to heaven. Read the story in your Bible: Matthew 25:1-13

Just like a car needs gasoline to run, you and I need God's help to "run" or live life each day. This fun song is really a prayer. We're asking God to provide what we need so that we can live and work for Him while we wait for Jesus to return.

Praise Signs

Use these simple movements as you worship with this song:

give: Hold both hands in front with palms down, fingertips and thumbs touching; move them up and out ending with your hands palms up.

lamp (candle): Hold your left hand up, palm forward; touch the base of your left hand with your right index finger; wiggle your left fingertips.

oil: Hold your left flat hand with fingers pointing right. Pinch your little-finger edge of your left hand with your right thumb and index finger, and pull down.

fisherman: Place your left hand above your right as if holding a fishing rod. Pivot your hands quickly up and backward.

seeking: Make a few circular motions across your face from right to left with a C hand.

serving: Hold both hands in front of your body with your palms facing up; alternate moving them back and forth.

Homemade Clay Oil Lamp

Homemade Clay Oil Lamp

Purchase polymer clay and candle wicking from a craft store. Polymer clay is a man-made material that remains pliable for long periods, but bakes or "cures" in any oven at a fairly low temperature to a hard, often pliable surface. You'll need a clump of clay about the size of a tennis ball. Press thumbs down into the middle and form a bowl. Pinch one end of the bowl so it looks somewhat like a gravy boat. Bake the lamp according to the instructions included with the polymer clay. Later, pour a small amount of olive oil into the lamp. Place a candle wick in the oil and light the wick. You can also shape the clay around a tea-light candle; remove the tea-light before baking the polymer clay.

A Lamp Unto My Path

Hide a treat or gift for each player. Players sit on the floor. Turn off the lights and turn on a flashlight. Give the flashlight to a player who will lead the others in search of the surprises hidden in the room. Afterwards, talk about how the light helped players see well. Discuss how God's Word helps us see things better, too.

#13

I Want To Walk With Jesus

I want to walk, walk, walk
I want to walk with my Jesus
I want to walk, walk, walk
I want to walk with my Jesus
I want to walk, walk, walk
I want to walk with my Jesus
Walk with Jesus everyday.

I want to love, love, love
I want to love my Jesus
I want to love, love, love
I want to love my Jesus
I want to love, love, love
I want to love my Jesus
Love my Jesus everyday.

Walking, talking, loving, praying
Walking, talking, loving, praying
Walking, talking, loving, praying
Walking, talking, loving, praying
Walk with Jesus everyday.

I want to walk, walk, walk
I want to walk with my Jesus
I want to walk, walk, walk
I want to walk with my Jesus
I want to walk, walk, walk
I want to walk with my Jesus
Walk with Jesus everyday.
Talk with Jesus everyday.
Love my Jesus everyday
Walk with Jesus everyday.

© Twin Sisters IP, LLC. Words and Music by Kim Mitzo
Thompson, Karen Mitzo Hilderbrand, Hal Wright.

Scripture Spotlight

3 John 4
I have no greater joy than to hear that my children are walking in the truth.

24/7 stands for 24 hours a day 7 days a week. This means all day everyday. Jesus wants us to love Him everyday. Imagine Jesus walking beside you during the school day. Pray and talk to Jesus everyday—not just on Sunday. Each day find someway to show Jesus that you love Him. This is harder to do than it sounds. Most kids and adults can be so busy with so many activities. You and I need to really work hard at remembering to walk, talk, and love Jesus on Monday, Tuesday, Wednesday, Thursday, Friday, and Saturday—not just on Sunday.

Praise Signs

Use these simple movements as you worship with this song:

walk: Hold both flat hands in front with palms down; imitate walking by alternately moving each hand forward.

talk: Move both index fingers back and forth from your lips.

love: Cross your arms and bring them close to your chest.

praying: Fold your hands to pray.

everyday: Place your right fist on the right cheek, palms facing the cheek, and rub it forward several times.

Jesus: Touch your left palm with your right middle finger; then touch your right palm with your left middle finger

Imagine

Imagine yourself talking to Jesus. Write a sentence to complete each "bubble. What do you think Jesus might say to you?

I was tempted...

I love you because...

I wonder why...

Would you please help...

Thank you for...

I Love To Take A Walk

#14

How I love to take a walk
along the street
And to say hello to the
people that I meet
And to watch the show of
their happy, happy feet
And I say to myself,
it's a miracle.

Hallelu, Hallelujah!
I sing as I walk along.
Hallelu, Hallelujah!
God has given me such a
happy, happy song

© Twin Sisters IP, LLC. Words and Music by Kim Mitzo
Thompson, Karen Mitzo Hilderbrand, Hal Wright.

Scripture Spotlight

Psalm 40:3
He put a new song in my mouth, a hymn of praise to our God.

Do you ever just feeling like singing? Sometimes I sing to myself while driving alone in my car. Sometimes a song just pops into my mind—I can hear it and am singing it to myself while taking a walk around the neighborhood. Often the song is a silly song—one that just makes me smile and laugh. Other times it's a praise or worship song—one that helps me tell Jesus how much I love Him! Next time you feel like singing, go ahead and sing. Don't be ashamed or embarrassed to sing. Let the song say what's in your heart—the feelings and thoughts you have deep inside you.

People, People Everywhere

Ask God to make you aware of people all around you. The next time you and your family walk around the neighborhood make an effort to say "Hello" to the people you meet along the way. Maybe stop in front of some houses and quickly pray for the family that lives inside. When you're at the mall rest for a few minutes at the food court and study the people that walk by. Look at their faces: some people will look happy and joyful and others may look sad or appear to be sick. Pray silently for the people you see. Or while waiting for your food at the restaurant, pray silently for the people around you. Remind yourself that God loves every person that you see! Ask God to show them how much He loves them!

Praise Signs

Use these simple movements as you worship with this song:

walk: Hold both flat hands in front with palms down; imitate walking by alternately moving each hand forward.

hello: Move your right hand in a small arc to the right from your forehead.

happy: Move both flat hands in forward circular movements with your palms touching your chest alternately.

say: Make a small forward circular movent in front of your mouth with your right index finger pointed left.

me: Point your right index finger toward your chest.

hallelujah: Clap once; then hold up both closed hands with your thumb and index fingertips touching. Make small circular movements.

sing: Bend your left arm in front of you. Swing your right hand back and forth over your left arm.

miracle: Move your open hands up and forward a few times with your palms facing out. Make a fist with both hands then tap the wrist of your right hand on your left wrist.

Letter Connections

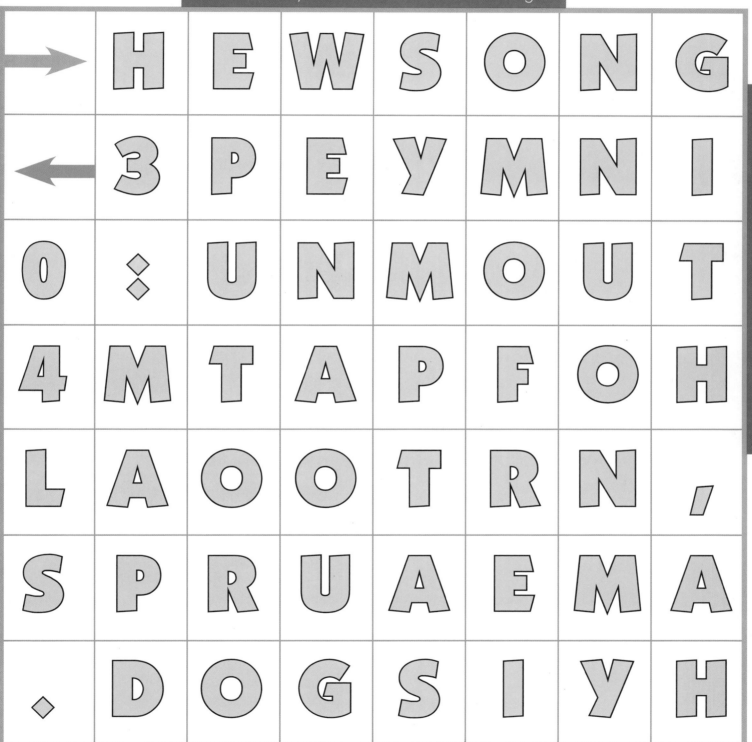

He put a new song in my mouth, a hymn of praise to our God. Psalm 40:3

Love, Love

#15

Love, love, love, love,
The Gospel in one word is love.
Love your neighbor as your brother,
Love, love, love.

Luke 10:27
He answered: " 'Love the Lord your God with all your heart and with all your soul and with all your strength and with all your mind'; and, 'Love your neighbor as yourself.' "

Love your neighbor. Who do you think of when you read or hear the word "neighbor"? If you're like me, you're thinking of the families who live in the houses on your street. And you're right. But when Jesus talked about neighbors he wasn't just talking about people who live in your neighborhood. When He said, "Love your neighbor," Jesus was really saying, "Love everybody." Now, that's tough to do. I try to remind myself that Jesus loves everybody—all the people in my neighborhood, my school, church, my country, and all the people in the world. And if Jesus loves that person than I can at least behave nicely and act lovingly toward that person, too. You try it. The next person you see, say to yourself, "Jesus loves him or her...and so do I."

Praise Signs

Use these simple movements as you worship with this song:

love:	Cross your arms and bring them close to your chest.
gospel:	While pointing your right index finger forward, slide the right hand across your left flat hand, fingertips to heel.
word:	Hold your left index finger up with palm facing right; then place your thumb and index finger of your right hand against it.
neighbor:	Hold your left curved hand away from your body, palms facing self; slide your right curved hand to behind your left hand. Next, with both palms facing each other, make a straight downward movement.
brother:	Pretend to grip the bill of a hat between your right fingers and thumb and then move it forward. Next, point both index fingers forward and bring them together side-by-side.

TIP – Tracks 15, 16, and 17 flow together as a great worship set!

God's Family

Make 5 sets of word cards. Write each of the following words on 5 separate index cards: WORSHIP, CARE, LOVE, PRAY, GIVE. To play, deal all the cards. Players simultaneously offer to trade 1 or 2 cards to other players until one player has collected all 5 of a word card. Before or after playing the game talk about why and how God's family worships and cares for others.

Grid Lock

God loves you and me. What does God want us to do since He loves us? Read the grid coordinates and fill in the letters on the blanks. The first number in the coordinate is always the bottom number.

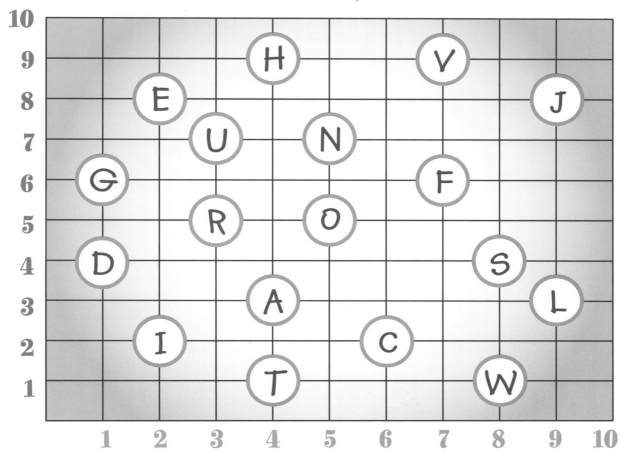

__ __ __ __ __ __ __ __ __ __ __ , __ __ __ __ __
1:4 2:8 4:3 3:5 7:6 3:5 2:2 2:8 5:7 1:4 8:4   8:4 2:2 5:7 6:2 2:8

__ __ __ __ __ __ __ __ __ __ __ __ , __ __
1:6 5:5 1:4 8:4 5:5 9:3 5:5 7:9 2:8 1:4 3:7 8:4   8:1 2:8

__ __ __ __ __ __ __ __ __ __ __ __ __ __
4:3 9:3 8:4 5:5 5:5 3:7 1:6 4:9 4:1 4:1 5:5 9:3 5:5 7:9 2:8

__ __ __ __ __ __ __ __ __ __ . 1 __ __ __ __ 4:11
5:5 5:7 2:8 4:3 5:7 5:5 4:1 4:9 2:8 3:5   9:8 5:5 4:9 5:7

Bible Songs

Scripture Spotlight

Everybody Ought To Know / He is Lord

Everybody ought to know
Everybody ought to know
Everybody ought to know
    who Jesus is.

He's the Lily of the Valley.
He's the Bright and
        Morning Star.
He's the Fairest of
        ten thousand.
Everybody ought to know!

On the cross He died
        for sinners
And His blood makes
        white as snow.
Loving, living, coming Savior,
He's the One you ought
        to know!

He is Lord, He is Lord,
He is risen from the dead
        and He is Lord.
Every knee shall bow,
        every tongue confess
That Jesus Christ is Lord!

Philippians 2:9-11
God exalted him to the highest place
    and gave him the name that is above every name,
[10]that at the name of Jesus every knee should bow,
    in heaven and on earth and under the earth,
[11]and every tongue confess that Jesus Christ is Lord,
    to the glory of God the Father

I love to worship Jesus at church with my friends and family. We sing, pray, and read God's Word together. Someday in heaven we will worship with EVERYONE who loves Jesus. I'm not sure what that worship will be like—but it seems like some will be singing, others will be shouting, and others will bow down on their hands and knees in front of the throne where Jesus is sitting. Whether we are singing, shouting, or bowing down, we will all be saying the same thing, "Jesus is Lord!" Lord is another word that means King. Imagine millions of people singing and shouting, "Jesus is King!" Now, that will be exciting.

Praise Signs

Use these simple movements as you worship with this song:

everybody: Close both hands; rub the knuckles and thumb of your right hand downward on your left thumb a few times; then with both palms facing each other, make a straight downward movement.

know: Tap your fingers of your right hand on your forehead a few times.

cross: Make a C with your right hand. Move your hand down and then left to right.

died: Begin with right palm down over left palm up; flip both hands.

blood: Hold your left hand, fingers spread in front of your chin. Move your right hand, fingers spread, down several times in front of your left hand.

snow: Place your thumb and fingertips of your right curved hand on your chest; then move it forward, touching your thumb and fingertips; then move both open hands downward while wiggling the fingers.

Savior: Cross closed hands on your chest. Rotate them to your sides, palms facing forward.

Lord: Make an L with your write hand near your left shoulder. Bring it down near your right waist.

risen: Hold your left hand flat, palm facing up. Bring your right V-fingers up from a palm-up position to stand on your left palm.

bow: Stand and kneel your right middle and index fingers on the palm of your left hand.

confess (acknowledge): Point the fingertips of both hands downward while touching your chest. Move both hands up and out until your fingers are pointing forward and your palms are facing up.

How Much Does God Love Me?

Follow these simple steps and discover
how much God Loves you!

 step 1 Fold down the top left corner of a piece of paper.

 step 2 Then fold down the top right corner.

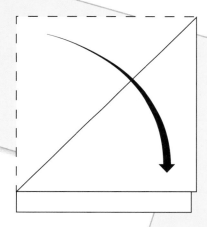

 step 3 Fold the left side over the right side.

 **step 4** Cut the paper along the fold line—about one-inch away from the fold.

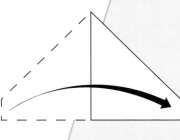

cut

discard

 step 5 Open up the folded part!

Read Romans 5:8 in your Bible.

Color Code

Color in only the boxes with a ☐ or ⬤.
The remaining boxes will reveal how much God loves you.

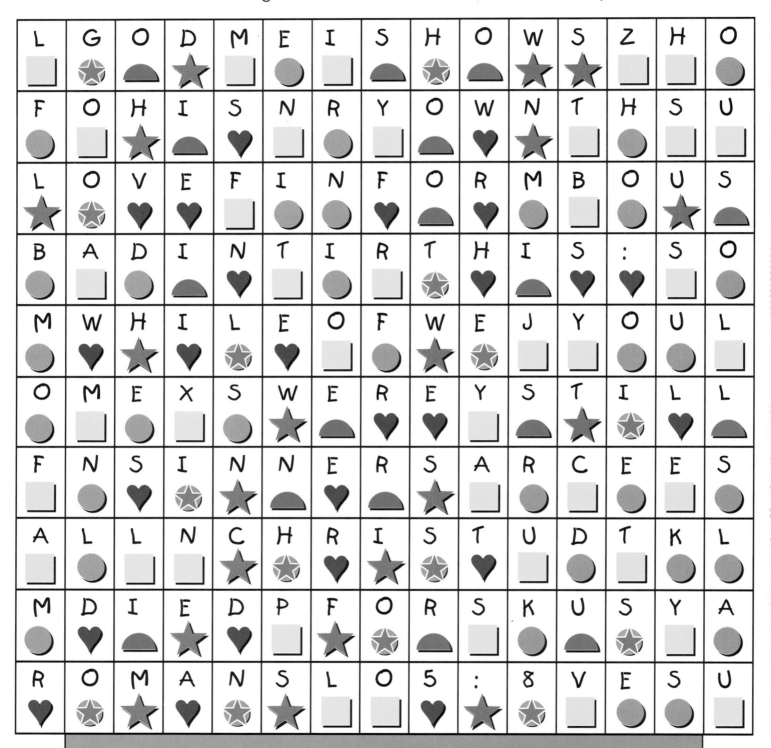

#17

When We All Get To Heaven

Sing the wondrous love of Jesus.
Sing His mercy and His grace.
In the mansions, bright
         and blessed,
He'll prepare for us a place.

When we all get to heaven,
What a day of rejoicing
         that will be!
When we all see Jesus,
We'll sing and shout the victory!

Onward to the prize before us.
Soon His beauty we'll behold.
Soon the pearly gates will open,
We shall tread the streets
         of gold.

When we all see Jesus,
We'll sing and shout the victory!

Scripture Spotlight

Revelation 5:13
Then I heard every creature in heaven and on earth and under the earth and on the sea, and all that is in them, singing:
   "To him who sits on the throne and to the Lamb
   be praise and honor and glory and power,
      for ever and ever!"

Do you ever wonder what heaven is like? People sometimes talk about streets of gold, bright lights, and big mansions in heaven. The truth is we don't really know exactly what heaven is like. But, one thing is for sure: Jesus is there. Jesus is sitting on a King's throne in the center of heaven. In fact, Jesus is what makes heaven heavenly!

This old song talks about the day when we all get to heaven...where Jesus is forever and forever.

Praise Signs

Use these simple movements as you worship with this song:

sing: Bend your left arm in front of you. Swing your right hand back and forth over your left arm.

wondrous: Place both closed hands at your temples with index fingertips and thumb tips touching. Flick both index fingers up simultaneously.

mercy: Move your right middle finger upward on your chest; then move your hand in a forward circle in front of your chest, palm down.

grace: Hold your right hand above your head, all fingertips touching; open your fingers and move your right hand down to lightly touch your head.

mansion (house): Form your point of a triangle at head level with both flat hands; move them apart and straight down, fingers pointing up.

prepare: Place both flat hands to your front and off to your left, palms facing and fingers pointing forward. Move both hands simultaneously to the right while moving them up and down slightly.

victory: Hold up both closed hands with your thumb tips and fingertips touching. Make small circular movements.

prize: With your palms facing each other, place both closed hands to your front. Move both hands forward in an arc.

gates: Point your fingertips of both flat hands together, palms facing in. Move your right hand back and forth a few times.

walk: Hold both flat hands in front with palms down; imitate walking by moving each hand forward.

open: Hold both flat hands side by side with your palms facing forward. Then slide both hands sideways in opposite directions.

day: Point your left index finger to right. Rest your right elbow on your left index finger with your right index finger pointing upward. Move your right arm in an arc from right to left.

bright: Hold both hands at chest level with your palms down. Open your hands as you move them up and to the sides with your palms forward.

Map to Heaven

Design a Map to Heaven! Start your adventure at the cross and end in heaven. Draw what you might experience along your way to heaven. For example, you might draw God's people, happy times, sad times, temptations, and God's Word.

HEAVEN

Bible Songs

#18

Praise The Lord Together

Praise the Lord together singing
Alleluia, Alleluia, Alleluia.
Praise the Lord together singing
Alleluia, Alleluia, Alleluia.
Praise the Lord together singing
Alleluia, Alleluia, Alleluia.
Praise the Lord together singing
Alleluia, Alleluia, Alleluia.
Praise the Lord together singing
Alleluia, Alleluia, Alleluia

Scripture Spotlight

Psalm 35:18
I will give you thanks in the great assembly; among throngs of people I will praise you.

Sometimes it's great to worship God all by yourself— all alone. It's quiet. You can sing what you want to sing! Pray out loud! Read quietly.

But, it's good to get together with other people who love God, too. You can worship with a small group of friends or family. You can worship with a large crowd of people. It can be exciting to hear others sing. You can pray together. You can read God's Word together.

The next time you go to church, remember you're going there to worship God with others who love Him too! That's a good thing to do.

Praise Signs

Use these simple movements as you worship with this song:

praise: Touch your right index finger to your mouth, then lightly clap your hands.

lord: Make an L with your right hand near your left shoulder. Bring it down near your right waist.

together: Place the knuckles of both closed hands together, move them in a semi-circle to your left.

singing: Bend your left arm in front of you. Swing your right hand back and forth over your left arm.

alleluia: Clap once; then hold up both closed hands with the thumb and index fingertips touching. Make small circular movements.

Praise Potato

Players stand or sit in a circle. Play praise music while players pass a foam ball or a stuffed animal. When the music stops, the player with the object must say one thing for which he or she is thankful.

Praise the Lord with Music

Unscramble the letters to spell musical instruments or things to do with music. Then unscramble the circled letters to learn what you can do with music. Read Psalm 150 in your own Bible for clues.

TEMPRUT _ _ _ _ ⟂ _ _ _

PRHA ⟂ _ ⟂ _ _

BNEIRTOUMA ⟂ _ _ _ ⟂ _ ⟂ _ _ ⟂

SSGNIRT _ _ _ ⟂ _ _ _

TLFUE _ ⟂ _ _ ⟂

SLAMCYB _ _ _ _ ⟂ _ _

DNCANIG ⟂ _ _ _ _ _ _

SNISNIG ⟂ _ _ _ _ _ _

◯ ◯ ◯ ◯ ◯ ◯   ◯ ◯ ◯   ◯ ◯ ◯ ◯ !

_ _ _ _ _ _   _ _ _   _ _ _ _

Homemade Praise Band

Have a Praise Parade for Jesus in your house, back yard, or maybe up and down the sidewalk. Attach crepe paper streamers to a dowel rod or baton. Gather your friends together and make these instruments—or use real musical instruments. Have fun marching, singing, and shouting in honor of Jesus, the King.

Box Guitar

Use an empty tissue box or shoe box. Have an adult cut an oval-shaped hole in the top of the box if the box doesn't already have one. Stretch several rubber bands around the box and over the hole. Put a pencil under the rubber bands, near the hole on one end. Tape a paper towel tube to the end of the box to make the neck of the guitar. Decorate the guitar with markers, crayons, and stickers.

Tambourine

Put a handful or two of dried beans, rice, or popcorn in a paper plate. Staple another paper plate securely on top of it. Decorate the plates with markers, crayons, stickers. Add ribbon or crepe paper streamers.

Finger Cymbals

Clean two frozen juice, baby food jar lids, or small jar lids. Place a small piece of masking tape on each side of both lids. Have an adult make 2 holes in the center of each lid, through the tape, using a nail. Thread a short piece of pipe cleaner through each hole, making a loop large enough to insert a finger. Twist at the end. Place a finger through the pipe cleaner and make music.

Soda Bottle Symphony

You'll need 8 20-ounce soda bottles to create a major scale. Label each bottle, 1 through 8. To make a major scale, add the following amounts of water. Then gently blow across the top of each bottle. Assign one or two bottles to friends or family!

Bottle 1	Do	7 ounces
Bottle 2	Re	9 1/2 ounces
Bottle 3	Mi	12 1/2 ounces
Bottle 4	Fa	14 ounces
Bottle 5	Sol	16 1/2 ounces
Bottle 6	La	17 1/2 ounces
Bottle 7	Ti	18 1/2 ounces
Bottle 8	Do	19 ounces

Homemade Praise Band

Trash Can Drum

Cut a square of canvas or heavy cloth about four inches larger than the diameter of a small trash can or bucket. Lay the cloth across the top of the can or bucket so that the edges hang evenly over the rim. Use Duct tape to tape the corners of the cloth to the can, working to stretch it as tight as possible. Tighten the drumhead by spraying the cloth with water and allowing it to dry. Use wooden spoons to play the drum.

Straw Oboes

Pinch and flatten one end of a paper or plastic drinking straw—paper straws will work better. Use scissors to cut an angle off each side of the flattened end. Lightly bend the remaining flaps. Place the straw into your mouth, positioning the flaps just inside your lips. Blow through the straw. Move the straw around to create the best musical note. Cut straws of different lengths to create different pitched tones.

Chimes

Attach several washers with string to a stick or ruler. Strike the washers with a spoon. If you want, paint the washers with different color nail polish before attaching them to the stick.

Mini Maracas

Decorate empty film canisters with vinyl tape. Have an adult cut a slit in the lids. Partially fill each canister with rice, beans, popcorn, or beads. Replace the lid and push in a craft stick.

Kazoo

Place a small piece of wax paper over one end of an empty toilet tissue roll. Secure the wax paper with a rubber band. Decorate the roll with crayons, colored pencils, markers, fabric, paints, or construction paper. Gently hum through the open end of your kazoo.

#19

Tell Me The Stories Of Jesus; Jesus Loves Even Me

Tell me the stories of Jesus
    I love to hear,
Things I would ask Him to
    tell me if He were here.
Scenes by the wayside,
    tales of the sea,
Stories of Jesus, tell them to me.

First let me hear how the
    children stood 'round His knee.
I shall imagine His blessing
    resting on me.
Words full of kindness,
    deeds full of grace,
All in the brightness of Jesus' face.

I am so glad that Jesus loves me.
Jesus loves me. Jesus loves me.
I am so glad that Jesus loves me.
Jesus loves even me.

I am so glad that Jesus loves me.
Jesus loves me. Jesus loves me.
I am so glad that Jesus loves me.
Jesus loves even me.

Jesus loves even me.

Scripture Spotlight

John 20:31
But these are written that you may believe that Jesus is the Christ, the Son of God, and that by believing you may have life in his name.

What are some of your favorite stories about Jesus? One of my favorites is when Jesus walked across the water to meet His friends who were in the boat. Oh, and I love when He was asleep in the boat and the weather was storming; Jesus woke up, said, "Peace," and the storm stopped! There are so many other stories—it's hard to choose a favorite. Jesus *told* stories to help everyone learn and understand how God wants people to live. His friends told stories about Jesus so that everyone would know that Jesus is God's Son. The next time you read or hear a story that Jesus told, ask yourself "What does God want me to learn?"

Praise Signs

Use these simple movements as you worship with this song:

tell me: Move both index fingers back and forth from your lips; then point your right index finger toward your chest.

stories: Link your thumbs and index fingers of both hands and pull them apart several times.

hear: Cup your right hand behind your right ear and turn your head a little to the left.

ask: Hold both curved hands in front, palms facing each other; then move both hands down and in toward your chest.

here: Hold both flat hands in front with palms facing up. Make circles in opposite directions.

words: Hold your left index finger up with palm facing right; then place your thumb and index finger of your right hand against it.

kindness: Place your right flat hand over your heart; then circle it around your left flat hand which is a short distance from your chest with palm facing in.

glad (happy): Move both flat hands in forward circular movements alternately touching your fingertips to your chest.

Word Wheel

Why did God write down in His Word so much of what Jesus said and did? Follow the word wheel to find the answer. Start with the circled letter on top of the wheel and read every other letter.

T___ ___ ___ ___

___ ___ ___ ___

___ ___ ___ ___, ___

___ ___ ___.

#20

I Want to Stop And Give My Lord Thanks

I want to stop
　　and give my Lord thanks.
I want to stop
　　and give my Lord thanks.
I want to stop
　　and give my Lord thanks.
For I have a grateful heart.

I want to stop
　　and give my Lord love.
I want to stop
　　and give my Lord love.
I want to stop
　　and give my Lord love.
For I have a loving heart.

I want to stop
　　and give my Lord praise.
I want to stop
　　and give my Lord praise.
I want to stop
　　and give my Lord praise.
For I love to praise my Lord.

© Twin Sisters IP, LLC. Words and Music by Kim Mitzo Thompson, Karen Mitzo Hilderbrand, Hal Wright.

Scripture Spotlight

Psalm 69:30
I will praise God's name in song and glorify him with thanksgiving.

Once while Jesus was having dinner with a friend, a woman came into the house. She stood behind Jesus, crying because she was happy! She poured expensive perfume on Jesus' feet. She even kissed Jesus' feet and wiped them with her hair. Some people thought the woman's actions were strange or wrong. But Jesus explained that the woman was really showing how much she loved Him. Jesus had forgiven her sins— forgetting what she had ever done wrong—and she was happy. Jesus said that anyone God has forgiven will also love God much! Read it yourself in Luke 7:36-50

Praise Signs

Use these simple movements as you worship with this song:

stop: Bring the little-finger side of your right hand flat down sharply on your left flat palm.

give: Hold both hands in front with palms down, fingertips and thumbs touching; move them up and out making flat hands, palms up.

Lord: Make an L with your right hand near your left shoulder. Bring it down to your right waist.

thanks: Touch the fingers of your right hand to your chin then bring them downward and outward.

praise: Touch your right index finger to your mouth, then lightly clap your hands.

Crossword Mix-Up

Fill in the missing words. Then unscramble the letters in circles and discover what Jesus said about the woman.

Jesus	woman	wipe	perfume	hair
dinner	cry	feet	sins	love
friends	happy	expensive	forgiven	kissed

" Jesus said,
_____ _____ _____ " • Luke 7:47

Bible Songs

21

Great Is Your Love

Great is your love!
　　It is higher than the heavens.
Your faithfulness reaches
　　to the skies!
Great is your love!
　　It is higher than the heavens.
Your faithfulness reaches
　　to the skies!
So I will love you, Lord,
　　and give you my praise.
I will lift up my hands
　　in joyous praise.
I will praise you Lord
　　with my voice and heart
Singing, "Lord you are true.
　　How great thou art!"

© Twin Sisters IP, LLC. Words and Music by Kim Mitzo
Thompson, Karen Mitzo Hilderbrand, Hal Wright.

Scripture Spotlight

Psalm 108:4
For great is your love, higher than the heavens;
*　　your faithfulness reaches to the skies.*

I sometimes play "How much do I love you?" with my daughter. I'll say to her, "McKenna, I love you a hundred thousand." And McKenna will reply, "Well, Dad, I love you five hundred million." Then I'll say, "I love YOU six trillion." And soon McKenna will make up some number like six-hundred-million-five-thousand-trillion-and-four-billion. It's a fun way to say to each other, "I love you more than you'll ever know!" And I always will love McKenna.

God loves you and me more than we'll ever understand! He loves you "six-hundred-million-five-thousand-trillion-and-four-billion". Write the largest number you can think of here:

Praise Signs

Use these simple movements as you worship with this song:

great: Move your flat open hands up and forward a few times with your palms facing out.

higher: Point your fingertips of both bent hands toward each other and raise both hands simultaneously.

heavens: Hold your right flat hand slightly above head level, palm facing in. Move it in arc from left to right.

faithfulness: Point both hands forward, your right hand over your left, and touching the thumbs and index finger. Move both hands forward while lightly tapping them together.

voice: Make a V with your right index and middle fingers. Move the V up your neck and under your chin.

joy: Move both flat hands in forward circular movements with palms touching your chest alternately.

sing: Bend your left arm in front of you. Swing your right hand back and forth over your left arm.

true: With your palm facing left, move your right index finger in a forward arc from your lips.

God's Heart Keepsake Basket

A heart-shaped basket is just the place to keep reminders of God's love. Photocopy the next page. Use colored paper, if possible. Fold on the dotted line. Cut along the solid lines. Fold both pieces in on the dotted line so that the lines don't show on your basket. Hold the two pieces together in a heart-shape. Weave the basket together by slipping the top folded strip around and through and around again. Do the opposite with the middle strip: through, around, and through. Finally, weave the bottom strip around and through and around again. If you want, make a handle from a strip of colored paper; glue the ends to the inside of the basket. On small strips of paper write several promises from God's heart that mean the most to you. Place the strips inside your "God's Heart Keepsake Basket" and store them in a very special place.

God promises to:

- Always love me
- Always forgive me
- Teach me the right way
- Hear me when I pray
- Help me when I'm scared

God's Heart Keepsake Basket Pattern

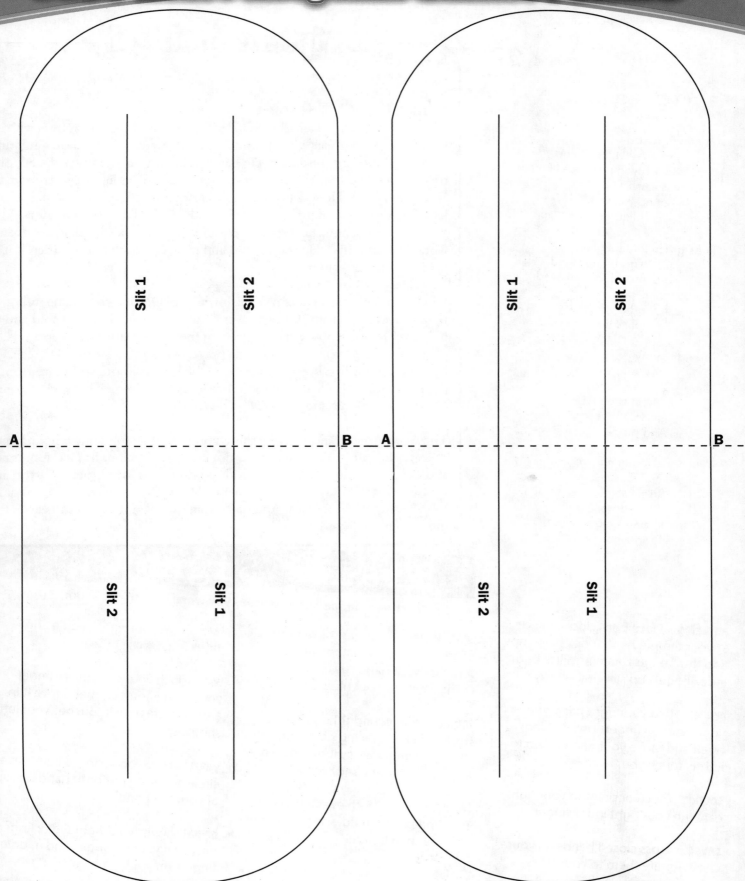

Bible Songs

Scripture Spotlight

#22

Amazing Grace

Amazing grace,
   how sweet the sound
     that saved a wretch like me!
I once was lost
   but now am found,
     Was blind but now I see.

'Twas grace that taught
   my heart to fear, and
     grace my fears relieved.
How precious did
   that grace appear
     the hour I first believed.

Through many dangers,
   toils, and snares
     I have already come.
'Tis grace hath brought
   me safe thus far,
     And grace will lead me home.

When we've been there
   ten thousand years,
     Bright shining as the sun,
We've no less days
   to sing God's praise
     Than when we'd first begun!

Ephesians 2:8
For it is by grace you have been saved, through faith—and this not from yourselves, it is the gift of God—

When John was 11 years old, he loved sailing big ships on the seas with his father. A few years later, John joined the navy and set sail on a fighting ship. But John was miserable. He hated being on the fighting ship. So, one night he left the ship without permission. The sailors and officers searched and found John. He was beaten and punished for leaving the ship. He hated living and working on that ship and he begged to be sent away. Soon, he was sent to be a servant on another ship—a ship that was even worse than the first. He was beaten and mistreated. One day, a friend of his family rescued John.

Later John became a captain of his own ship. On one voyage, he was trying to steer his ship through a very violent storm. He was scared and he prayed, "Lord, please have mercy on me." Later, after the storm was over, John began to think about his prayer during that storm. He realized how good God had been to him. Soon, he learned more and more from the Bible. John finally understood that Jesus loved him. That's when John Newton wrote this song, *Amazing Grace.*

The word "grace" means something good given to someone who may not deserve the gift. John Newton did not always love God. In fact, John said and did many things that make God sad. But God loved John Newton and was willing to forgive him. John thanked God for being so kind to him. John learned to love Jesus. And he couldn't wait until he got to heaven to meet Jesus.

Praise Signs

Use these simple movements as you worship with this song:

amazing: Place both closed hands at your temples with index fingertips and thumb tips touching. Flick both index fingers up simultaneously.

grace: Hold your right hand above your head, all fingertips touching; open and move your hand down to lightly touch your head.

sound: Touch or point to your right ear with your right index finger.

saved: Cross closed hands on your chest. Rotate them to your sides, palms facing forward.

lost: Hold your fingertips of both hands together, palm up; then separate your hands by dropping them down and opening the fingers.

found: Hold your right open hand in front with palm facing down. Bring the index finger and thumb together as you raise your hand.

blind: Point to both eyes with your right index and middle fingers, fingers straight then bended.

see: Point your right middle and index fingertips at the eyes.

we: Touch your right index finger on your right shoulder; then move it in a semi-circle until it touches your left shoulder.

years: Move both closed hands in a circle and rest your right hand on top of your left hand.

begun: Twist your right index finger between your left index and middle fingers on your left hand.

Amazing What?

Some words in the hymn *Amazing Grace* may be new or strange.
Draw a line from each word to what the word means in this song.

Words	Meanings
Amazing	Rescued
Grace	God's goodness and kindness
Saved	Wonderful, awesome
Wretch	I don't understand!
Blind	An unhappy person.
See	Difficult experiences
Fears	I'm afraid God doesn't love me!
Relieved	Worship God
Snares	Now I understand!
"There"	I'm not afraid anymore!
Praise	Heaven

Scripture Spotlight

#23

My Jesus, I Love Thee

My Jesus, I love Thee,
    I know Thou art mine.
For Thee all the follies of sin
    I resign.
My gracious Redeemer,
    my Savior art Thou.
If ever I loved Thee,
    my Jesus, 'tis now!

I love Thee because
    Thou hast first loved me,
    and purchased my pardon
    on Calvary's tree.
I love Thee for wearing
    the thorns on Thy brow.
If ever I loved Thee, my
    Jesus, 'tis now!

In mansions of glory
    and endless delight
    I'll ever adore Thee
    in heaven so bright.
I'll sing with the
    glittering crown on my brow.
If ever I loved Thee,
    my Jesus, 'tis now.

If ever I loved Thee,
    my Jesus, 'tis now.

1 John 4:10
This is love: not that we loved God, but that he loved us and sent his Son as an atoning sacrifice for our sins.

Did you tell someone today that you love them—maybe mom, dad, grandma, grandpa, a special aunt or uncle, or even a brother or sister? I love it when my kids say, "Dad, I love you!" It makes me feel so good inside. Sometimes they'll say why they love me. "Dad, you are fun to play with." Or, "Dad, you do so many nice things for me."

Jesus likes to hear you say, "I love you." He likes to hear why you love Him, too. "Thank you, Jesus for dying on the cross. I love you." Or, "Thank you, Jesus, for promising that I can live with you forever. I love you."

My Jesus, I Love Thee is an old song called a hymn. It's really a poem. We don't use some of the words today: "Thee" and "Thou" mean "You" or "God"; "Art" means "are."

Read and sing this hymn with someone. Count how many times you say, "I love you"? Try to find the reasons why the writer loves Jesus.

TIP – Tracks 21, 22, and 23 flow together as a great worship set!

Praise Signs

Use these simple movements as you worship with this song:

sin: Point both index fingers toward each other with palms facing self. Move them simultaneously in up-out-down circles.

resign: Make a C with your left hand. Place your right index and middle fingers in and out of your left C hand.

pardon: Stroke the lower part of your left flat hand several times with your right fingertips.

Calvary's tree (cross): Make a C with your right hand. Move your hand down and then left to right.

crown: Make a C with both hands and pretend to place the crown on your head.

now: Hold both bent hands to the front at waist level, palms up. Drop both hands a short distance.

Fill In The Hymn

Fill in the missing letter to spell words from the hymn. When all the letters are used, look in the boxes to discover a message.

M⬜INE

M⬜ESUS

R⬜SIGN

⬜IN

THO⬜

THORN⬜

SAV⬜OR

CA⬜VARY

CR⬜WN

LO⬜ED

TR⬜E

⬜IS NOW

⬜EAVEN

ADOR⬜

REDE⬜MER

Use these words:

adore
Calvary
crown
heaven
Jesus
loved
mine
My
Redeemer
resign
Savior
sin
thorns
Thou
tis now
tree

Bible Songs
Scripture Spotlight

#24

What A Mighty God We Serve

What a mighty God we serve.
What a mighty God we serve.
Angels bow before him.
Heaven and earth adore him.
What a mighty God we serve.

Psalm 145:4
One generation will commend your works to another; they will tell of your mighty acts.

In the winter I love watching heavy snow fall and carefully cover each and every branch of all the trees. Each spring, I'm amazed when the snow melts away and the tiniest flowers begin to poke through the ground! I can't make snow and I can't make a flower! But God can and does! What a mighty God we serve!

On another sheet of paper, make a list of the mighty things God has done! Think hard. Can you write at least 10 things? 25? 50?

Praise Signs

Use these simple movements as you worship with this song:

mighty: Move both fists firmly forward and downward.

God: Point your right index finger upward. Move your hand back and down, fingers pointing up, and your palm facing left.

we: Touch your right index finger on your right shoulder; then move it in a semi-circle until it touches your left shoulder.

Serve: Hold both hands in front of your body with your palms facing up; alternate moving them back and forth.

angels: Touch your shoulders with your fingertips. Then point your fingertips outward and flap them a few times.

bow: Stand and kneel your right middle and index fingers on the palm of your left hand.

heaven: Hold both hands in front, fingers pointing up, palms facing your body. Move both hands in a circle and end with your hands crossed at your forehead.

earth: Grasp the back of your left closed hand with your right index finger and thumb; pivot your right hand from left to right.

Worship: Close your left hand over your right closed hand and move them slowly toward yourself.

Mighty God Word Search

Circle these words that describe God. Each of these words can remind you of how powerful God is! Ask someone to explain words that you don't understand.

Most High	Creator	Ruler	Strong Tower
Living God	King of Glory	Lord	Shield
King of Kings	Fortress	Rock	Almighty
Strength	Awesome	Refuge	Eternal

```
M O S T H I G H X O T S Y C
N L I V I N G G O D R T O R
E T E R N A L M A N F R U E
T H E X C I E V O U S E R A
K I N G O F G L O R Y N A T
I M I G A H T O N O S G W O
N A R U L E R R D C J T N R
G K E F M R L D R K Q H A E
O R F R I I R A E F U O M S
F I U E G K F O R T R E S S
K O G N H E R E D A M M O H
I L E M T R Q U A L L O S I
N I A D Y T O A W E S O M E
G T R O S T I N G M O R S L
S Y S T R O N G T O W E R D
```

Bible Songs

Scripture Spotlight

#25

A Mighty Fortress Is Our God

A mighty fortress is our God,
    a bulwark never failing.
Our helper He amid the flood
    of mortal ills prevailing.
For still our ancient foe
    doth seek to work us woe.
His craft and power are great
    and armed with cruel hate
On earth is not his equal.

Did we in our own strength confide
    our striving would be losing.
Were not the right man on our side,
    the man of God's own choosing.
Dost ask who that may be?
    Christ Jesus, it is He,
Lord Sabaoth His name,
    from age to age the same,
And He must win the battle!

That Word above all earthly pow'rs,
    no thanks to them abideth.
The Spirit and the gifts are ours
    through Him who with us sideth.
Let goods and kindred go
    this mortal life also.
The body they may kill.
    God's truth abideth still.
His kingdom is forever!

A mighty fortress is our God.
A mighty fortress is our God.

TIP – Tracks 24, 25, and 26 flow together as a great worship set!

Psalm 46:1
God is our refuge and strength, an ever-present help in trouble.

A Mighty Fortress Is Our God is a hymn. About the year 1527 Martin Luther wrote the hymn after reading Psalm 46. He wrote the words in German. Today, Christians all over the world sing this hymn. It has been translated into over 20 other languages. The hymn is a great reminder that God is strong. God is in control.

Look up these verses in your Bible. Do you think that Martin Luther was thinking of these Scriptures when he wrote this hymn?

1 Peter 1:3-7
1 Peter 5:8-9
Romans 8:38-39

Praise Signs

Use these simple movements as you worship with this song:

mighty: Move both fists firmly forward and downward.

God: Point your right index finger upward. Move your hand back and down, fingers pointing up, and your palm facing left.

helper: Place your right closed hand on your left flat palm. Lift both hands together. Then drop both flat hands down, palms facing each other.

foe (enemy): Point your index fingers toward each other. Pull them apart sharply. Then drop both flat hands down, palms facing each other

craft (work): Touch your shoulders with your fingertips. Then point your fingertips outward and flap them a few times.

win: Bring both hands together while forming a fist. Place your right hand on top of your left hand. Then hold up the right hand with your thumb and index finger touching and make small circular movements.

right: With your right hand above your left hand, point both index fingers forward. Lightly tap your right hand on your left hand.

man: Touch the thumb of your right open hand on your forehead, then on your chest.

kingdom: Move your right hand from your left shoulder to your right waist. Then circle counterclockwise your right flat hand over your left flat hand.

A Mighty What?

Many words in the hymn may be new or sound strange. Memorizing and understanding the words will help you trust God no matter what is happening in our world.

Mighty	very big, very strong
Fortress, bulwark	a strong place where you are protected
Flood of mortal ills	many hard problems, sin, bad things
Our ancient foe	God's enemy
Work us woe	God's enemy wants to create problems
On earth is not his equal	No one on earth is strong enough to face God's enemy
In our own strength confide	Try to fight God's enemy by yourself
The right man on our side	Jesus—the Son of God
From age to age the same	Jesus is just as strong today
He must win the battle	The things we have and the people we love
God's truth abideth	God's Word is always true
His kingdom is forever	God wins! His Kingdom will never end

The Faithful Wordfinder

Find each of the following words.

BATTLE	ABIDETH	MIGHTY	POWER	FOREVER
WORD	STRENGTH	ANCIENT	FAILING	JESUS
GIFTS	WIN	AGETOAGE	EARTH	TRUTH
EQUAL	KINGDOM	FORTRESS	SPIRIT	FOE

```
G W J E S E S E F O R E V E R M
E I A E A E T F S T R R E S
E N I T O G T O J E S U S S
S P I R I T E R B A T T L E
G P O P I M S T R E N G T H A
T H G I F T S R O E Q U L A
F O E K I N G E T A T U E O
A B I D E T H S W N G O K F
E M I G H T Y S E O G E I A
E G P S N D A I N N R F N O
Q F F O T E C N I H H D G R
U O O T W N A L C T E W D P
A R R P A E I R U I C E O W
L E T H S A R R T D E H M I
I R R A F W T T D H I C S T
```

Bible Songs

#26

Kum Ba Yah

Kum ba yah, my Lord,
    kum ba yah.
Kum ba yah, my Lord,
    kum ba yah.
Kum ba ya, my Lord,
    kum ba yah.
Oh, Lord, kum ba yah.

Someone's crying, Lord,
    kum ba yah.
Someone's crying, Lord,
    kum ba yah.
Someone's crying, Lord,
    kum ba yah.
Oh, Lord, kum ba yah.

Someone's laughing, Lord,
    kum ba yah.
Someone's laughing, Lord,
    kum ba yah.
Someone's laughing, Lord,
    kum ba yah.
Oh, Lord, kum ba yah.

Someone's singing, Lord,
    kum ba yah.
Someone's singing, Lord,
    kum ba yah.
Someone's singing, Lord,
    kum ba yah.
Oh, Lord, kum ba yah.

Someone's praying, Lord,
    kum ba yah.
Someone's praying, Lord,
    kum ba yah.
Someone's praying, Lord,
    kum ba yah.
Oh, Lord, kum ba yah.

1 Peter 5:7
Cast all your anxiety on him because he cares for you.

Jesus was leaving the city, surrounded by crowds of people. The crowds of people didn't pay attention to the blind beggar man sitting on the ground near a building. The blind man was crying out in a loud voice, "Jesus! Have mercy on me!" Some people in the crowd told the man to be quiet. But he shouted even louder. Jesus heard his shouts and stopped. Jesus asked that blind man what he wanted. The blind man said, "Jesus, I want to see!" And Jesus healed the blind man. Read it for yourself in your Bible: Mark 10:46-52.

The blind man was shouting for Jesus to come by because he knew Jesus would show love and compassion. "Kum Ba Yah" means "come by here." People have sung this simple song for a long time. It's a way of say, "Come by here, Jesus. We need you."

Praise Signs

Use these simple movements as you worship with this song:

come: Point both index fingers toward each other and circle them toward your body.

here: Hold both flat hands in front with palms facing up. Circle them foward and out..

Lord: Make an L with your right hand near your left shoulder. Bring it down near your right waist.

someone: Hold your right index finger up with palm facing forward and shake it lightly back and forth.

crying: Move one or both index fingers down your cheeks from underneath your eyes a few times.

laughing: Start near the corners of your mouth, move both index fingers upward—and smile.

singing: Bend your left arm in front of you. Swing your right hand back and forth over your left arm.

praying: Fold your hands to pray.

My Handy Prayer Guide

Your fingers and thumb can be a handy dandy reminder of how to pray. The thumb and each finger are reminders of someone or something to pray for. Hold out your hand and take a few moments each day to pray. Or decide to pray the thumb on Mondays, index finger on Tuesdays, middle finger on Wednesdays, ring finger on Thursdays, and pinky finger on Fridays!

Thumb

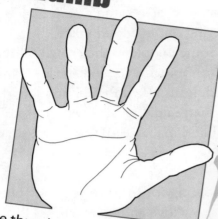

The thumb is the strongest finger on your hand. **Give thanks to God** for being so strong and so mighty.

Index

This is the pointing finger. **Pray for people who teach you** and help you: parents, teachers, pastors and others.

Middle

This is the tallest finger on your hand. **Pray for leaders** in our city, our state, our country, and the world.

This is the farthest finger on your hand. **Pray for someone who lives far away**—maybe a missionary who has visited your church.

Pinky

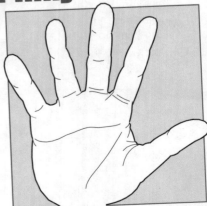

Ring

The fourth finger is the weakest finger on your hand. **Pray for those who are sick, poor, and needy.**

Grid Lock

Break the code to discover what God wants you to do whenever you're worried.

	1	2	3	4	5
✴	P	7	J	W	L
●	E	Y	L	B	R
⬠	C	I	F	1	S
★	M	N	5	O	:
♥	U	T	X	A	H

⬠:1 ♥:4 ⬠:5 ♥:2   ♥:4 ●:3 ●:3   ●:2 ★:4 ♥:1 ●:5

♥:4 ★:2 ♥:3 ⬠:2 ●:1 ♥:2 ●:2   ★:4 ★:2   ♥:5 ⬠:2 ★:1

●:4 ●:1 ⬠:1 ♥:4 ♥:1 ⬠:5 ●:1   ♥:5 ●:1   ⬠:1 ♥:4 ●:5 ●:1 ⬠:5

⬠:3 ★:4 ●:5   ●:2 ★:4 ♥:1 • ⬠:4   ✴:1 ●:1 ♥:2 ●:1 ●:5   ★:3 ★:5 ✴:2

Answer: Cast all your anxiety on Him because He cares for you. 1 Peter 5:7

The Old Testament Song

#27

I'm gonna learn the books of the Bible.
I'm gonna learn the books today.
I'm gonna learn the books of the Bible.
So when my preacher says to turn to Obadiah,
Ezra, Job, or Nehemiah,
I'll know to turn to Jeremiah
for I'm learning all the books today.

Genesis, Exodus, Leviticus, Numbers
Deuteronomy, Joshua, Judges, Ruth and Samuel—there are two of these!
First and Second Kings, First and Second Chronicles,
Ezra, Nehemiah, Esther, Job, Psalms and Proverbs, Ecclesiastes,
Then there's Song of Songs, Isaiah, Jeremiah, Lamentations, Ezekiel,
Daniel, Hosea, Joel and Amos, Obadiah, Jonah, Micah, Nahum,
Habakkuk, Zephaniah, Haggai, Zechariah—we're almost through—
The last is Malachi.

I have just learned the books of the Bible
I have just learned those books today.
I have just learned the books of the Bible.
I just can't wait 'til Sunday!

Old Testament Book Search

Find and circle each Old Testament Book. The names may be found horizontally, vertically, diagonally, foward, or backward.

Genesis	1 Samuel	Esther	Lamentations	Micah
Exodus	2 Samuel	Job	Ezekiel	Nahum
Leviticus	1 Kings	Psalms	Daniel	Habakkuk
Numbers	2 Kings	Proverbs	Hosea	Zephaniah
Deuteronomy	1 Chronicles	Ecclesiastes	Joel	Haggai
Joshua	2 Chronicles	Song of Songs	Amos	Zechariah
Judges	Ezra	Isaiah	Obadiah	Malachi
Ruth	Nehemiah	Jeremiah	Jonah	

```
D S B R E V O R P U S A 1 1 S A M U E E E
L A E S U H S O B A D I A H E S N I K C
H I N Z U E A L I S A I I H L V S P C C
Y I E I G D E N J O S H U A C L G S X L
M I N D E U O A O G C S K N I A N A E E
O I U D M L L X L J K Z O H N M O L S S
N J K A I M E R E J U U E S O E S M T I
O S S L E U M A S 2 K D O P R N F S H A
R 1 E S S S R U T H K M C U H T O S E S
E M J E R E M I A H A E H I C A G G R T
T I G E N E S I S T B N A A 1 T N N R E
U B E I H C A L A M A E E G U I O I H S
E L E V I T I C U S H G S G N O S K A K
D E J O E L Z G L J O B O A H N P 1 I H
2 C H A I A S I E H R G H S S R M M L
N K E M A E R S I 2 C H R O N I C L E S
R N I B U N E Z K Z E C H A R I A H H E
O O H N M H O S E M S Y H A C I M M E H
H E O O G U A J Z E I S S R E B M U N P
L S J N O S N N E A O E K H A M L G N T
```

The New Testament Song

#28

Matthew, Mark, Luke and John, Acts, and next is Romans,

First and Second Corinthians, Galatians, and Ephesians,

Philippians, Colossians, First and Second Thessalonians,

First and Second Timothy, Titus and Philemon,

Hebrews, next is James, First and Second Peter,

First John, Second John, Third John,

Jude and Revelation.

New Testament Mix-up

The name of each New Testament book is mixed up.
Draw a line from each mixed up name to the correct name.

SNAMOR	MATTHEW
SNAITALAG	MARK
STCA	LUKE
WEHTTAM	JOHN
NHOJ	ACTS
SNAIHTNIROC1	ROMANS
EKUL	1CORINTHIANS
SNAISSOLOC	2 CORINTHIANS
SNAIHTNIROC2	GALATIANS
KRAM	EPHESIANS
SNAINOLASSEHT1	PHILIPPIANS
SNAIPPILIHP	COLOSSIANS
YHTOMIT1	1THESSALONIANS
SNAISEHPE	2 THESSALONIANS
SUTIT	1 TIMOTHY
SWERBEH	2 TIMOTHY
SNAINOLASSEHT2	TITUS
NOMELIHP	PHILEMON
YHTOMIT2	HEBREWS
NOHJ1	JAMES
SEMAJ	1 PETER
EDUJ	2PETER
RETEP1	1 JOHN
NHOJ3	2 JOHN
NOITALEVER	3 JOHN
RETEP2	JUDE
NHOJ2	REVELATION

Bible Book Activities

What Comes Next? What Comes First?

Call out a book of the Bible. The other player must call out one of the books of the Bible that comes either right before or right after in the order of the books. You can play this game in a large group: players who answer correctly continue to play; players who answer incorrectly sit out. The last player standing wins!

Bible Book Speed Race

Try to recite all the books of the Bible as quickly as possible as a group, with each player saying only one book at a time. The first player says "Genesis" and the next "Exodus" and so on until "Revelation" is reached.

Bible Library!

Collect a set of 66 books or magazines. Make a cover for each book or magazine out of construction paper. Write one book of the Bible on each cover. For more fun, use books and magazines of different sizes to correspond with the Bible book size. For example, you might use a thick dictionary for the book of Psalms and a very thin magazine for the book of Jonah. Make two complete sets for team play!

To play:

1. **Stack the books of the Bible in order—or begin with just one testament. Eventually race against a timer to see how quickly you can stack the books.**

2. **Mix up all the books of the Bible. Separate the books into two piles: Old Testament and New Testament**

3. **Remove one or two Bible books. Players must determine which book(s) are missing.**

Pocket-size Guides to the Books of the Bible

Cut the two guides on the solid lines. Fold each guide accordian-style on the dotted lines. Give a guide to a friend.

2

Genesis — Ge
Exodus — Ex
Leviticus — Lev
Numbers — Nu
Dueteronomy — Dt
Joshua — Jos
Judges — Jdg
Ruth — Ru
1 Samuel — 1Sa
2 Samuel — 2Sa

OLD TESTAMENT

3

1 Kings — 1Kt
2 Kings — 2Kt
1 Chronicles — 1Ch
2 Chronicles — Nu
Ezra — Ezr
Nehemiah — Ne
Esther — Est
Job — Job
Psalms — Ps
Proverbs — Pr

OLD TESTAMENT

4

Ecclesiastes — Ecc
Song of Songs — SS
Isaiah — Isa
Jeremiah — Jer
Lamentations — La
Ezekiel — Eze
Daniel — Da
Hosea — Hos
Joel — Joel
Amos — Am

OLD TESTAMENT

5

Obadiah — Ob
Jonah — Jnh
Micah — Mic
Nahum — Na
Habakkuk — Hab
Zephaniah — Zep
Haggai — Hag
Zechariah — Zec
Malachi — Mal

OLD TESTAMENT

2

Genesis — Ge
Exodus — Ex
Leviticus — Lev
Numbers — Nu
Dueteronomy — Dt
Joshua — Jos
Judges — Jdg
Ruth — Ru
1 Samuel — 1Sa
2 Samuel — 2Sa

OLD TESTAMENT

3

1 Kings — 1Kt
2 Kings — 2Kt
1 Chronicles — 1Ch
2 Chronicles — Nu
Ezra — Ezr
Nehemiah — Ne
Esther — Est
Job — Job
Psalms — Ps
Proverbs — Pr

OLD TESTAMENT

4

Ecclesiastes — Ecc
Song of Songs — SS
Isaiah — Isa
Jeremiah — Jer
Lamentations — La
Ezekiel — Eze
Daniel — Da
Hosea — Hos
Joel — Joel
Amos — Am

OLD TESTAMENT

5

Obadiah — Ob
Jonah — Jnh
Micah — Mic
Nahum — Na
Habakkuk — Hab
Zephaniah — Zep
Haggai — Hag
Zechariah — Zec
Malachi — Mal

OLD TESTAMENT

POCKET-SIZE Guide To The Books Of The Bible

NAME _____

1

NEW TESTAMENT

Hebrews	Heb
James	Jas
1 Peter	1Pe
2 Peter	2Pe
1 John	1Jn
2 John	2Jn
3 John	3Jn
Jude	Jude
Revelation	Rev

8

NEW TESTAMENT

Ephesians	Eph
Philippians	Php
Colossians	Col
1 Thessalonians	1Th
2 Thessalonians	2Th
1 Timothy	1Ti
2 Timothy	2Ti
Titus	Tit
Philemon	Phm

7

NEW TESTAMENT

Matthew	Mt
Mark	Mk
Luke	Lk
John	Jn
Acts	Ac
Romans	Ro
1 Corinthians	1Co
2 Corinthians	2Co
Galatians	Gal

6

POCKET-SIZE Guide To The Books Of The Bible

NAME _____

1

NEW TESTAMENT

Hebrews	Heb
James	Jas
1 Peter	1Pe
2 Peter	2Pe
1 John	1Jn
2 John	2Jn
3 John	3Jn
Jude	Jude
Revelation	Rev

8

NEW TESTAMENT

Ephesians	Eph
Philippians	Php
Colossians	Col
1 Thessalonians	1Th
2 Thessalonians	2Th
1 Timothy	1Ti
2 Timothy	2Ti
Titus	Tit
Philemon	Phm

7

NEW TESTAMENT

Matthew	Mt
Mark	Mk
Luke	Lk
John	Jn
Acts	Ac
Romans	Ro
1 Corinthians	1Co
2 Corinthians	2Co
Galatians	Gal

6

Bible Book Builder

The object of the game is to build each section of the Bible in the correct book order. The player who plays all of his or her cards first is the winner.

1. Old Testament LAW
2. Old Testament HISTORY
3. Old Testament POETRY
4. Old Testament MAJOR PROPHETS
5. Old Testament MINOR PROPHETS

6. New Testament GOSPELS
7. New Testament HISTORY
8. New Testament LETTERS TO CHURCHES
9. New Testament LETTERS TO INDIVIDUALS
10. New Testament GENERAL LETTERS
11. New Testament PROPHECY

How to Play

Deal 7 cards to each player. Place the remaining cards face down in the center of the table. Each player arranges the cards in his or her cards under the categories listed above. On your turn play as many cards as possible. The section title card must be played first and the Bible book cards played in correct order. End your turn by picking the top card from the draw pile and playing the card, if possible. Once all the cards in the draw pile have been used, players must play or pass.

Old Testament LAW	Genesis	Exodus
	OT Law	OT Law
Leviticus	Numbers	Deuteronomy
OT Law	OT Law	OT Law

This page was intentionally left blank for the Bible Book Rummy activity to be completed.

Old Testament HISTORY	Joshua	Judges
	OT History	OT History
Ruth	1 Samuel	2 Samuel
OT History	OT History	OT History
1 Kings	2 Kings	1 Chronicles
OT History	OT History	OT History
2 Chronicles	Ezra	Nehemiah
OT History	OT History	OT History
Esther	Old Testament POETRY	Job
OT History		OT Poetry
Psalms	Proverbs	Ecclesiasties
OT Poetry	OT Poetry	OT Poetry
Song of Songs	Old Testament MAJOR PROPHETS	Isaiah
OT Poetry		OT Major Prophets
Jeremiah	Lamentations	Ezekiel
OT Major Prophets	OT Major Prophets	OT Major Prophets

This page was intentionally left blank for the Bible Book Rummy activity to be completed.

Daniel	Old Testament MINOR PROPHETS	Hosea
OT Major Prophets		OT Minor Prophets
Joel	Amos	Obadiah
OT Minor Prophets	OT Minor Prophets	OT Minor Prophets
Jonah	Micah	Nahum
OT Minor Prophets	OT Minor Prophets	OT Minor Prophets
Habakkuk	Zephaniah	Haggai
OT Minor Prophets	OT Minor Prophets	OT Minor Prophets
Zechariah	Malachi	New Testament GOSPELS
OT Minor Prophets	OT Minor Prophets	
Matthew	Mark	Luke
NT Gospels	NT Gospels	NT Gospels
John	New Testament HISTORY	Acts
NT Gospels		NT History
New Testament LETTERS TO CHURCHES	Romans	1 Corinthians
	NT Letters to Churches	NT Letters to Churches

This page was intentionally left blank for the Bible Book Rummy activity to be completed.

2 Corinthians	Galatians	Ephesians
NT Letters to Churches	NT Letters to Churches	NT Letters to Churches
Philippians	**Colossians**	**1 Thessalonians**
NT Letters to Churches	NT Letters to Churches	NT Letters to Churches
2 Thessalonians	New Testament **LETTERS TO INDIVIDUALS**	**1 Timothy**
NT Letters to Churches		NT Letters to Individuals
2 Timothy	**Titus**	**Philemon**
NT Letters to Individuals	NT Letters to Individuals	NT Letters to Individuals
New Testament **GENERAL LETTERS**	**Hebrews**	**James**
	NT General Letters	NT General Letters
1 Peter	**2 Peter**	**1 John**
NT General Letters	NT General Letters	NT General Letters
2 John	**3 John**	**Jude**
NT General Letters	NT General Letters	NT General Letters
New Testament **PROPHECY**	**Revelation**	
	NT Prophecy	

This page was intentionally left blank for the Bible Book Rummy activity to be completed.

Sign Language Praise Signs Index

adore (worship)	18	everybody	42
age to age (forever)	64	everyday	36
all	16	eyes	32
alleluia (hallelujah)	47	faces	22
always (forever)	6	faithfulness	55
amazing (wondrous)	58	family	64
angels	62	feet	32
appreciate	18	fisherman	34
ask	51	foe (enemy)	64
battle	64	forever (always)	28
begun	58	fortress	64
bless	16	found	58
blind	58	gates	45
blood	42	give	34
body	64	glad (happy)	51
bow down	18	go	24
bright	45	God	18
brother	40	good	18
calls (says)	24	gospel	40
Calvary's tree (cross)	60	got (have)	30
careful	32	grace	45
children	11	great	55
Christian	28	guide	18
clap	14	hallelujah	11
cleanse (pardon)	26	hands	32
climb	22	happy	26
come	24	have (got)	30
confess (acknowledge)	42	hear	51
craft (work)	64	heart	26
cross	42	heaven	24
crown	60	Heavenly Father (God)	18
crying	67	heavens (sky)	22
day	45	hello	38
died	42	helper	64
down	30	here	51
ears	32	higher	55
earth	62	Holy Spirit	18
evening	9	I (me, my)	18

Sign Language Praise Signs Index

I love you	14		resign	60
inside	18		right	64
Jesus	9		risen	42
joy (happy)	30		saved	58
kill	64		Savior	42
kindness	51		say (call)	24
kindred (family)	64		see	58
kingdom	64		seeking	34
know	42		serve (serving)	9
lamp (candle)	34		shout	6
laughing	67		sin	26
live	28		sing	6
look	22		sky (heavens)	22
Lord	16		snow	42
lost	58		someone	67
love	9		soul	16
man	64		sound	58
mansion (house)	24		Spirit (Holy Spirit)	6
me (I, my)	16		stop	53
mercy	45		stories	51
mighty	62		talk	36
miracle	38		tell me	51
morning	9		thank	9
mountain	22		together	47
my (I, me)	16		true	55
name	16		turn	22
neighbor	40		us (we)	18
noontime	9		victory (win)	45
now	60		voice	55
oil	34		walk	36
open	45		welcome	24
pardon (cleanse)	26		win (victory)	64
peace	30		wondrous (amazing)	45
praise	9		word(s)	40
pray	6		worship	14
prepare	45		yes	24
prize	45		you	14
rejoice	6			

Scripture Memory Activities

IN THE

REJOICE

LORD!

Memory Balloons

Blow up a balloon for each word in a Bible memory verse. Write one word on each balloon, and then deflate the balloons. Players blow up a balloon and tape it to the wall or hang it from a string. Players put the words in the correct order. Pop one balloon at a time and recite the verse.

Scripture Memory Circle

Players stand or sit in a circle. Play praise music while passing a foam ball or a bean bag, but players must say the memory verse before they pass the object. When the music stops the child who is holding the bean bag must sit down or step out of the circle.

1 2 4 3

Bible 4 Square

Draw a four-square court with sidewalk chalk or use masking tape to play indoors. You'll need at least four players and one playground ball. One player stands in each of the four squares. Other players line up behind square #4. Players say one word in the Bible memory verse and bounce the ball to another player. That player must say the next word in the verse and bounce the ball to another player. Continue until you've recited the entire verse. If a player misses the ball or a word, that player rotates to the end of the line. Players in the remaining squares advance, and the next player in line enters square #4. You can also review the books of the Bible in the same way!

Scripture Memory Activities

Bible Memory Concentration

Write the words of a Bible memory verse on index cards, one to three words on each card. Make two identical sets. Mix up both sets of cards and place them facedown on the table. Players take turns turning over two cards at a time, keeping them if the cards match. If the cards do not match, return the cards facedown. Play until all the cards have been collected. Then put both sets of cards in the correct order.

PRAISE THE LORD

O MY SOUL

O MY SOUL

PRAIS THE LOR

What's Wrong?

Write several Bible verses on index cards. However, purposely misspell names, omit words, switch the word order, add words, provide incorrect references, etc. Looking in their Bibles players must discover and correct the mistakes.

ORDL ADN VSAIOR

OICJE

LOVE IS YOUR GREAT FOR

I WILL _____ YOUR LOVE

Word Catchers by Gra

by God

Write words or phrases of a scripture verse on wide masking tape. Cut the phrases apart. Players tape the words or phrases to the front of their shirts. One player, "It," tries to tag the other players. When players are tagged they must line up in the correct word or phrase order. For more challenging play, "It" must tag and/or line up the tagged players in the correct order.

Scripture Memory Verses

Philippians 4:4

Rejoice in the Lord always. I will say it again: Rejoice!

Psalm 92:1-2

It is good to praise the LORD and make music to your name, O Most High, to proclaim your love in the morning and your faithfulness at night.

Psalm 8:2

From the lips of children and infants you have ordained praise.

Acts 3:8

He jumped to his feet and began to walk. Then he went with them into the temple courts, walking and jumping, and praising God.

Psalm 103:1

Praise the LORD, O my soul; all my inmost being, praise his holy name.

Psalm 107:1

Give thanks to the LORD, for he is good; his love endures forever.

Philippians 3:14

I press on toward the goal to win the prize for which God has called me heavenward in Christ Jesus.

John 14:6

Jesus answered, "I am the way and the truth and the life. No one comes to the Father except through me."

Scripture Memory Verses

James 5:13

Is any one of you in trouble? He should pray. Is anyone happy? Let him sing songs of praise.

John 3:16

For God so loved the world that he gave his one and only Son, that whoever believes in him shall not perish but have eternal life.

Philippians 4:7

And the peace of God, which transcends all understanding, will guard your hearts and your minds in Christ Jesus.

Ephesians 5:15

Be very careful, then, how you live—not as unwise but as wise.

Matthew 25:13

Therefore keep watch, because you do not know the day or the hour.

3 John 4

I have no greater joy than to hear that my children are walking in the truth.

Psalm 40:3

He put a new song in my mouth, a hymn of praise to our God.

Luke 10:27

He answered: " Love the Lord your God with all your heart and with all your soul and with all your strength and with all your mind'; and, 'Love your neighbor as yourself.'"

Scripture Memory Verses

Philippians 2:9-11

God exalted him to the highest place and gave him the name that is above every name, that at the name of Jesus every knee should bow, in heaven and on earth and under the earth, and every tongue confess that Jesus Christ is Lord, to the glory of God the Father.

Revelation 5:13

Then I heard every creature in heaven and on earth and under the earth and on the sea, and all that is in them, singing: "To him who sits on the throne and to the Lamb be praise and honor and glory and power, for ever and ever!"

Psalm 35:18

I will give you thanks in the great assembly; among throngs of people I will praise you.

John 20:31

But these are written that you may believe that Jesus is the Christ, the Son of God, and that by believing you may have life in his name.

Psalm 108:4

For great is your love, higher than the heavens; your faithfulness reaches to the skies.

Ephesians 2:8

For it is by grace you have been saved, through faith—and this not from yourselves, it is the gift of God.

1 John 4:10

This is love: not that we loved God, but that he loved us and sent his Son as an atoning sacrifice for our sins.

Psalm 145:4

One generation will commend your works to another; they will tell of your mighty acts.

Scripture Memory Verses

Psalm 46:1

God is our refuge and strength, an ever-present help in trouble.

1 Peter 5:7

Cast all your anxiety on him because he cares for you.

2 Timothy 3:16

All Scripture is God-breathed and is useful for teaching, rebuking, correcting and training in righteousness...

Psalm 119:9-11

[9]How can a young man keep his way pure? By living according to your word. [10]I seek you with all my heart; do not let me stray from your commands. [11]I have hidden your word in my heart that I might not sin against you.

Psalm 69:30

I will praise God's name in song and glorify him with thanksgiving.

Psalm 100

[1]Shout for joy to the LORD, all the earth. [2]Worship the LORD with gladness; come before him with joyful songs. [3]Know that the LORD is God. It is he who made us, and we are his; we are his people, the sheep of his pasture. [4]Enter his gates with thanksgiving and his courts with praise; give thanks to him and praise his name. [5]For the LORD is good and his love endures forever; his faithfulness continues through all generations.